The Archetypes of Carlos Fuentes

The Archetypes of Carlos Fuentes

From Witch to Androgyne

by

Gloria B. Duran

1980

Archon Books

Library of Congress Cataloging in Publication Data

Durán, Gloria.
  The Archetypes of Carlos Fuentes: from Witch to
Androgyne.

A rev. and enl. English version of the author's La magia y
las brujas en la obra de Carlos Fuentes, published 1980.
  Bibliography: p. 225.
  1. Fuentes, Carlos—Knowledge—Occult sciences.
2. Witchcraft in literature.   I. Title.
PQ7297.F793Z63   1980   863   80-12285
ISBN 0-208- 01775-5

© Gloria B. Durán 1980

First published 1980 as an Archon Book, an imprint of
The Shoe String Press, Inc., Hamden, Connecticut
06514

Contents

Contents 7

Prologue

For too long, the Latin American novel has been criticized by specialists who sought to read it only as a document about a violent and tragic reality. Thus, the works of some of its most important authors (Rulfo and Arguedas, Ramos and Guimarães Rosa, Fuentes and García Márquez, Cabrera Infante and Vargas Llosa) have served as a pretext for pseudo-historical or pseudo-sociological essays stubbornly involved with the reality to which these novels undeniably allude.

Fuentes has been one of the favorite authors of these myopic readers. Disdaining, in his earlier work, the visible signals of a mythical view, ignoring its symbolic imagery, the politically committed critics used to praise his work as a perfect example of realistic literature, only to attack it later for a (supposed) symbolic deviation that began to take place in the sixties.

The initial praise and the current criticism seem equally unjustified. From the very beginning, Fuentes has been a writer; that is to say, a man who uses the written word in order to convey not a direct vision of what happens in reality, but who uses the written word (and is used by it) in order to communicate its multiple meanings. To read him as if he were only a realistic narrator is worse than not to read him at all.

All this, which is so obvious today, after *Holy Place, Change of Skin, Birthday*, and *Terra Nostra*, was not so obvious in the early sixties, when Fuentes had already published *Aura* and *The Death of Artemio Cruz*. An article which I wrote in 1963 served as a pretext for some good readers and critics of Fuentes to ridicule "my" obsession with symbols and myths. Now Fuentes's work has created his own criticism. Among its best practitioners, one finds Gloria Durán, whose book deals with one of the principal themes in Fuentes's work. It was my privilege to have contributed from the beginning to the preparation of this study. During one of the courses I taught at Yale University some years ago, where the theme of witches in the new Hispanic American novel (Bianco, Donoso, and Fuentes were the main authors) was briefly mentioned, Gloria Durán contributed her knowledge of Russian literature and in particular, of that spellbinding protagonist of *The Queen of Spades*, to our discussion. I believe it was there that this admirable investigation was begun.

Thanks to her, it is possible now to read Fuentes with new insight, to go directly to the heart of certain symbolic configurations in his work and discover there the presence (explicit or latent) of the underlying myth of the enchantress. Fuentes, himself, in a letter to Gloria Durán, has provided the anecdotal key to his obsession: his discovery, at the age of six, of some striking images of the Mexican empress, Carlotta. They awakened something in him which motivated, through the serpentine path of other texts and other experiences, his fiction.

On the other hand, the theme of the enchantress is one of those which are fundamental to the Western mythic experience. In studying Michelet, Roland Barthes (*Michelet par lui-même* [Paris: Éd. du Seuil, 1954],

p. 65) has conveyed this experience in words which must
be quoted:

> La Sorcière est, au moyen âge, dépositaire de la
> médecine, qui est pour Michelet une technique de
> pénétration. Elle possède d'ailleurs tous les car-
> actères d'un principe mâle: elle est une essence
> (comme l'*homunculus* des spermatistes) et elle est
> un acte d'ouverture. Son nom féminin ne doit pas
> égarer (L'Histoire n'est-elle pas elle aussi, fausse-
> ment, au féminin?): plus que femme, elle est ma-
> trone, c'est-à-dire sexe superlatif et complet, ré-
> unissant le pouvoir mâle et le pouvoir femelle. (On
> verra plus tard que chez Michelet cet ultra-sexe est
> à dominante féminine.)

Michelet's conception of the enchantress exaggerates,
and, at the same time, expresses in accordance with very
personal obsessions, the vast symbolism of this fabulous
figure. Certain elements (that power of penetration, that
sexual nature which is at once superlative and complete)
are recognizable in some of Fuentes's enchantresses.
This is especially so in the protagonist of *Holy Place,*
who dominates sexually both men and women, and who,
in her supreme triumph, is presented as the current symbol of Mexico, making obsolete the traditional super-
macho, Pancho Villa.

The theme has infinite variations. We should thank
Gloria Durán for developing it not only with such penetration, but with a viewpoint that has reestablished the
reading of Fuentes's works within a truly challenging
context.

Yale University   *Emir Rodríguez-Monegal*

Author's Preface

The present study began about ten years ago as an article, eventually grew into a thesis, was later published—with many modifications—as a book in Spanish (*La magia y las brujas en la obra de Carlos Fuentes* [Mexico, D.F.: University of Mexico Press, 1976]) and now, with a certain amount of pruning, grafting, and the addition of three new chapters, it becomes the first work in English to deal exclusively with the body of Fuentes's novels which have been translated into our language.

Today Fuentes lives in Princeton, New Jersey. His fictional works are being published in English almost as soon as they appear in Spanish. It is high time that a public that does not read Spanish have easy access to critical appraisals of this highly popular author.

Admittedly, this study makes no pretense of being a general analysis of his work. One of the reasons for this, perhaps, is that the engagé, polemical Fuentes had become the nearly exclusive subject for commentary by Mexican critics during the first decade of his active career. Fuentes himself consciously abetted this highly political focus on his works. In his early enthusiastic support of Fidel Castro and other revolutionaries, in newspaper articles and public statements, he continually projected the image of the intellectual leftist critic of the Mexican Establishment. This politicized image of Fuentes was also being faithfully reflected by American Hispanists.

And yet as early as his first published work, an untranslated collection of short stories of 1954, it was obvious that Fuentes was extraordinarily attracted by his mythical Aztec heritage. In all of his novels (with the exception of *The Good Conscience*, a realistic novel in the style of Galdós) there is an unmistakable vein of the mythical. And in at least five major novels the occult vein rises to the surface, enveloping the entire work.

Of course, when this study was begun, Fuentes's obsession with myth was not the obvious fact that it is today. For those who wish to explore further Fuentes's mythological world of the unconscious there is available today a wealth of criticism, in both English and Spanish, some of which is noted in the bibliography. There is also an excellent bibliography on Fuentes by Richard M. Reeve that appeared in *Hispania* (53 [1970]: 597–652) and was later included in the first volume of his complete works (*Obras completas* [Madrid-Mexico: Aguilar, 1974]). Yet when the first five chapters of the present book were written, this criticism had not yet appeared. (That which is most relevant to my own focus I have since incorporated into these first five chapters.)

However, to my knowledge, there has been nothing written, either by Fuentes or any of his critics, that in any way destroys the validity of my original observation, namely, that there is at least one sorceress, implicit or explicit, who dominates nearly every one of Fuentes's novels. This sorceress or witch stands as a guide to the subterranean world of the unconscious, which is the world that has increasingly preoccupied Fuentes. Therefore, a study of the witch and her multiple mutations—

the final one being that of androgyne—is critical to an understanding of Fuentes's works as a whole.

My assumption is that the reader of this study is probably more or less familiar with most of Fuentes's novels and of course with the author himself. For this reason no highly detailed biography of Carlos Fuentes will be given. (Although Fuentes decries its interpretation and even its facts, such a biography can be found in English in Daniel De Guzmán's *Carlos Fuentes* [New York: Twayne Publishers, 1972]). For those who read Spanish, Fuentes has provided his "biographical data" in volume one of the already referred to *Obras completas*. Nevertheless, for the sake of any clarity that the writer's life may shed on his work, I include the following resumé of the above mentioned autobiography, brought up to date through conversations with Fuentes.

Biographical Data

Fuentes was born on 11 November 1928, under the sign of Scorpio. This is the first information provided in his biographical data, and the inclusion of his astrological position suggests a strong attraction to the occult in this otherwise cooly rational writer and diplomat. Even the matter of his date of birth has been clouded by a certain amount of speculation because of Fuentes's own statements—a subject that will be dealt with more fully in our discussion of *Aura*.

The Fuentes family tree has roots in Germany, the Canary Islands, Spain, and, of course, Mexico. Fuentes's own peripatetic existence could be due not only to the life-style imposed on the immensely popular writer, but to the habit of travel acquired as the son of a Mexican diplomat. During the six years (1934–40) his father, Rafael Fuentes Boettiger, was attached to the Mexican Embassy in Washington, D.C., Carlos learned English which he speaks and writes nearly as well as Spanish. (His first, unpublished novel was written in English.) As a child his favorite writers were Mark Twain, Jules Verne, R. L. Stevenson and Alexandre Dumas.

His obvious taste for adventure, natural in an imaginative youth, must have been nourished by trips to Canada, Chile, Argentina, Brazil, etc. In his eagerness to associate himself with historic or terrifying events, Fuentes tells us that he made his first trip to New York on the next to last voyage of the *Morro Castle*. Similarly, he frames himself in a world surrounded by the great figures of politics, literature, and later the theatre and the movies. Among those luminaries he mentions as friends or acquaintances are Nehru, Castro, ex-president Cardenas of Mexico, Tito, Nasser, Sukarno, Ilya Ehrenburg, Echeverría, and Neruda, and his acquaintances among English and other foreign writers and artists are equally dazzling. Yet fortunate for his talents as a writer able to portray all classes of society is his acknowledged passion for night life, and the world of prostitutes, hangers-on, burlesque dancers, mariachis, and all those types normally considered "bohemian" in his own middle-class milieu.

As a man, Fuentes is a powerhouse of irrepressible enthusiasm, humor and wit. Yet he can be ruthless in protecting his own privacy, and he has a penchant for creating enemies as easily as friends.

He points out that whereas for many years he was persona non grata in the United States because of his leftist tendencies, he has also suffered criticism in the Soviet Union because of his outspoken attack on Soviet intervention in Czechoslovakia. Like his close friend and mentor Octavio Paz, he has consistently fought for the intellectual's prerogative of avoiding blind commitment to any ideology. Also, following in the footsteps of Paz, he has both accepted and rejected important diplomatic posts. Fuentes served during the administration of Echeverría (whom he strongly supported) as ambassador to France from 1975 to 1977. But when Diaz-Ordaz (the president held responsible for the massacre of students in 1968) was appointed ambassador to Madrid, Fuentes resigned his own position in protest.

Nevertheless, Fuentes has not recaptured his role of idol for Mexico's leftist, intellectual youth, the role that he held in the sixties. His brief association with the establishment has tainted him forever in the eyes of many Mexican critics. Besides, now more than fifty, he is no longer young and therefore no longer considered a spokesman for Mexico's youth. With the years he has become increasingly cosmopolitan, increasingly interested in the personal, existential problems that face the individual at middle age. The parochial and political ills of Mexico have been integrated into a far broader canvass, and the surrealistic images that he now paints have left many of his former admirers with a feeling of bewilderment and betrayal.

Yet whatever acclaim Fuentes has lost at home has perhaps been compensated for by the growing body of his readers and critics of his work in translation. Eventually, he says, he plans to settle in Paris (the Mecca of so many Latin American intellectuals). In the meantime, he has been earning his living not only as a writer (of novels, plays, film scripts, and journalistic articles), but also as a professor in the United States. For the last few years he has given lectures at numerous American universities and taught at Princeton, Columbia, and the University of Pennsylvania. In 1978 the University of South Carolina held a two-day symposium devoted to his work.

One of Fuentes's life-long obsessions (other than witches and magic) has been the movies. He counts Luis Buñuel and Shirley MacLaine among his intimate friends. Another was Rita Macedo, the Mexican actress who became his first wife in 1959. Since 1973, however, he has been married to Sylvia Lemus, also a writer and journalist. Today far from the hurly-burly of Mexican politics, he is superficially indistinguishable from any other suburban paterfamilias commuting to his various pedagogical posts from the little oasis of Princeton, New Jersey.

Yet no period is of very long duration with Fuentes. Sooner or later, one suspects, he will tire of Princeton. He is a warehouse of projects. (Among his unfulfilled ambitions, he once told me, was that of being a political cartoonist, something he does secretly as the ghost cartoonist for one of his friends.)

Fuentes is a man of many faces, many roles. But he is best known as one of our most prolific, most influential Latin American writers. He handles pornographic passages and metaphysical disquisitions with equal facility. He probably takes sadistic delight in posing constant enigmas for his critics. His own "biographical data" deal only with the persona of Fuentes, Fuentes as a statesman and writer. Significantly absent is any detailed reference to the important women in his life; his mother, his sister, his first or second wife. For the anima in Fuentes's life, we must look to his fictional writings (and also to one of his letters that appears in the appendix to this volume). Since we know so little about the "inner" Fuentes, perhaps the only safe prediction that can be made is that he will continue his torrential literary production, probably for both economic and psychological reasons. He has recently told me that his latest completed novel is called *Los Heredia*.

"Could it be realistic?" I wondered. The title made me think of *The Good Conscience*, which was supposed to be the first volume of a trilogy that never appeared.

Fuentes laughed, undoubtedly pleased to have misled still another one of his critics. "You should know better," he said. "It's magic, of course. More magic."

Introduction

The Importance of Mythology for Carlos Fuentes

In July 1964 Carlos Fuentes in an article in *Siempre* ("La nueva novela Latinoamericana," *Siempre* 579 (1964):4) suggested the probable future direction of the Latin American novel. At that time Fuentes was already well known as one of Mexico's young engagé writers who in two major works (*Where the Air is Clear* and *The Death of Artemio Cruz*) had attacked the power structure in his country and the betrayal of the Mexican revolution. Yet even then for Fuentes the realistic, documentary novel, the grand panorama of history and geography, was a thing of the past. The future task for his generation, he said, was to mythify and personalize, to develop a new type of novel that would be both Latin American and universal.

Fuentes's analysis of the course of Latin American literature was further amplified in an interview in July 1966 with Emir Rodríguez-Monegal which was published in the magazine *Mundo Nuevo* ("La situación del escritor en America Latina," *Mundo Nuevo* 1 (1966):

5–21). At this time he divided Latin American culture
and literature into three chains or tangential circles,
those of the Utopia, the Epic, and the Myth. The first
was the world of Thomas More put into practice. The
entire continent was discovered as, and considered to
be, a kind of Utopia. (Since this Utopia was destroyed
by the concrete necessities of history which turned it
into the epic of Cortés, we may assume that only such
works as those of Columbus, Pané, and Pérez de Oliva
belong to the Utopia period.) According to Fuentes, the
largest, most important circle must be the epic one since
he considers this to be the basic form in which Latin
American literature has clothed itself up to the present.
But now, he said, the epic possibility is exhausted—and
there remains only the mythical alternative which is "a
possibility of choosing this past, of leaving this past
which is just history, vagrant history, in order to enter
into a dialectic, which is to make history, and to fashion
it out of myths . . ."[1] Like his friend, the essayist and
poet Octavio Paz, Fuentes has come to distrust history
as a tool for understanding man. According to Paz, man
is not in history, but "is history"; his character is not
only the result of the past but itself explains historical
circumstances.[2] For Paz as for Fuentes, myth is often
more understandable, more "real" than history. It is
Fuentes (in the interview with Rodríguez-Monegal) who
says, "through myth we reenact the past, we reduce it
to human proportions,"[3] and predicts that his own work
will be increasingly influenced by the mythical approach.

Yet for some reason Fuentes's growing interest in
myth seems to hold most of his critics at bay. Whereas
the bibliography on *Where the Air is Clear* (1958), *The
Good Conscience* (1959), or *The Death of Artemio Cruz*
is enormous, fewer critics have occupied themselves
with *Aura* (published in 1962, the same year as *The
Death of Artemio Cruz*), his first thoroughly magic novel,

and even fewer with *Holy Place, Change of Skin* (both published in 1967) or *Cumpleaños* (published in 1969 but untranslated).

At first sight these newer books by Fuentes offered a very divergent appearance from his politically engagé writings and pronouncements. Even such commentaries on *Aura*, for example, as that of Luis Harss and Barbara Dohmann (*Into the Mainstream*, [New York: Harper and Row, 1967]) almost dismiss it as a sort of fairy tale and express wonder that the author himself should attach so much importance to it. Only a few critics like Joseph Sommers and Emir Rodríguez-Monegal have dug deeply enough in *Aura* to fathom Fuentes's very serious purpose in writing it.

This lack of understanding, especially on the part of Mexican critics, has created a certain bitterness in Fuentes. Sommers reports that in an interview with the author, Fuentes complained that among his critics there is too little concern for serious, up-to-date evaluation of contemporary literature. "He lamented the general absence of sound, critical commentary. The result (according to Fuentes) is an atmosphere of gossip, personal competitiveness, and false parochial values. As a consequence, the Mexican writer must await evaluation from abroad to gain a true perspective on his work."[4]

It is under such circumstances that the foreign critic is emboldened to approach so formidable a writer as Carlos Fuentes, one whose current literary production is so swathed in myth that the exact meaning of some of his works is almost impossible to understand or explain without constant reference to the world of myths. However, since the world of myths is anything but parochial, the foreign critic may be at least as perspicacious as the Mexican one in an analysis of Fuentes's recent novels. And unlike both the Mexican critics and admirers who originally stamped Fuentes as a serious, realistic writer, we are not apt to regard his new trend as merely a frivolous detour.

Neither is the particular aspect of myth that I propose to investigate, the role of witches in Fuentes's works, of a superficial or marginal nature. The archetypal figure of the witch has appeared in nearly all of his literary production, starting from his first published collection of short stories. The witch can be found even in such realistic novels as *The Death of Artemio Cruz*. In other works, such as *Aura* or *Holy Place*, she is the central character.

The present study proposes to trace the development of this mythical figure from her initial appearance through to *Terra Nostra*, Fuentes's last important novel. Fuentes himself describes her as an "obsession," "an obsession with what Octavio Paz calls 'the enchantress, the witch, the white serpent.' "[5] Speaking of his witches in *Where the Air is Clear* to a reporter for the French literary magazine *Le Figaro Littéraire*, Fuentes reveals that "I went to the sorceresses, keep this in mind, because I wanted to or needed to; I didn't go with paper to take notes."[6] However, it is my intention to go beyond the largely personal explanation for the enchantress that Fuentes himself offers. I shall first attempt to explore the attraction of this mythological creature for the human psyche in general, as only in this way can one understand her importance to Fuentes and to other writers; for the "witch phenomenon" continues from earliest times until the present, in Mexico, in the United States, and indeed all over the world. Only through the historical and psychological perspective, as well as the literary one, can we fully appreciate the role of the sorceress in Fuentes's views on love, politics, and such philosophical matters as time, reality, and life itself.

The sorceress incarnates Fuentes's abiding metaphysical and social preoccupations. As a symbol of transformation, she hovers over his work from the very beginning. Chameleon-like, she is nevertheless always detectable. Little by little, Fuentes's witch "changes skin" and metamorphosizes into the hermaphrodite, symbolizing as such a state of wholeness which expresses an obsessive nostalgia in modern man. In this study we shall trace the development of Fuentes's archetypal female from her gothic inception to her metaphysical consummation in *Terra Nostra,* and her anticlimatic fragmentation in *The Hydra Head.*

I
The Witch as a Historical, Psychological and Social Theme

Earlier Witches in Spanish Literature

Carlos Fuentes is, of course, not the first modern writer to concern himself with witches or enchantresses. (For the moment we shall use the terms interchangeably.) If at first we consider only Spanish literature, we will see that a witch gives her name to one of the first Spanish novels, which was written by Fernando de Rojas and published in 1499. *La Celestina* was as famous for being "herbolera" and "bruja" as for her activities as a go-between (which also have always been considered a classical part of the witch's occupations).[1]

Perhaps the next most famous witch in Spanish literature is Fabia, of Lope de Vega's *El Caballero de Olmedo*. William McCreary in his study of the work remarks that "in Lope's design Fabia's image is integral to the anatomy of the tragedy. Through her he activates all the Medieval-Renaissance terror of the black arts, the occult sciences," yet "whether or not Lope himself believed in witches and their arts cannot be answered." McCreary goes on to outline a detailed study of witchcraft, its practices, persecutions, and general impact on

the Renaissance. "It was," he writes, "a part of the tem-
per of the times, as much as Communism or Capitalism
or any other -ism is of ours."[2]

But this historical approach does not explain the continued popularity of the witch into the nineteenth century, with the famous witches of Goya and Bécquer, and,
in world literature, of Pushkin, Henry James, and H.
Rider Haggard. There are Romantic witches—and witches
of our enlightened, neo-positivistic period. Though a
literary critic, McCreary therefore realizes that there
must be a psychological explanation of the "witch phenomenon" as well as a historical one.

Psychological Explanations of the Witch

In his chapter entitled "Alcahuetería and Brujería"
("Pandering and Witchcraft"), McCreary writes on
page 57:

> Every society needs an explanation for evil that is
> more concrete than the abstract and abstruse prin-
> ciples offered by its dominant philosophies or theol-
> ogies. Perhaps more than explanation, what is called
> for is a material focal point toward which man can
> project all that he holds to be perverse, repugnant,
> destructive and opposed to righteousness. . . . The
> less intellectually gifted . . . demand an enemy to
> complement the abstraction. Unlike Augustine, most
> men do not have the courage to confess the presence
> of a dark sector in their souls.

It is this "dark sector" in our own souls that is not a
historically unique phenomenon. Although the witch-
hunts of the Renaissance and the seventeenth century
are over, the "dark sector" within us is very much the

same as when it was defined by Lope, Shakespeare, Goya, etc. The difference today is that the witch as a scapegoat is no longer so socially useful, since we now have developed a theory of the unconscious "to provide an acceptable release, both amoral and 'aresponsible,' for the destructive coefficient in man's nature . . ."[3] Witches, therefore, by and large have receded into the world of dreams and the realm of literature, which they still continue to haunt as the symbol of evil.

The Modern Witch

And yet the witch has not completely disappeared as a social phenomenon. Our newspapers and magazines increasingly point to new interest in witches (particularly among the young) to a degree that almost amounts to a religious revival. In an article in the *New York Times*, Andrew M. Greeley, a Roman Catholic priest and sociologist, discusses a student organization called WITCH (Women's International Terrorists Corps from Hell), which describes itself as the continuation of a "neolithic religion that worshipped the great earth goddess until it was replaced by Christianity."[4]

Father Greeley himself describes the organization as "a combination of the put-on and the serious, the deliberately comic and the profoundly agonized, of the bizarre and the holy." The same description might well be applied to Fuentes's treatment of the witch. In both cases, as well as in the extraordinary new interest in astrology, and other studies of the occult, we are facing a contemporary disenchantment with science, a search for the meaningful and the sacred, in an increasingly grey and impersonal world. Lay sociologists like Alvin Toffler attribute the current craze for astrology, cults and other irrational attractions to a reaction of *Future Shock* (New

York: Random House, 1970), which is an inability to cope with the speed of social and technological change. Feeling betrayed by science and logic, the individual seeks refuge in the security of smaller groups. Liberty and the constant necessity for making bewildering choices are willingly sacrificed for reintegration into a womb-like environment cemented by the irrational or unconscious desires.

Father Greeley compares the witch movement to the hippie culture, but today we might extend the comparison to any cultist groups, including such suicidal ones as that of the Reverend Jones. They all seem to be rooted in "an existential dissatisfaction with the way things are."[5] On the social plane they correspond to the revival of mythology and the interest in the unconscious on the literary plane. In other words, Fuentes's obsession with witches and other mythological phenomena is very much a product of our times.

Cultural Heroes of the Unconscious

According to Father Greeley, one of the cultural heroes of the new occult movements is Mircea Eliade. According to Emir Rodríguez-Monegal, Mircea Eliade is also one of the cultural heroes of Carlos Fuentes. Like Eliade in his mythological and anthropological studies, Fuentes too investigates such exotic fields as transvestitism, fetishism, initiation rites, or the hermaphrodite, but largely within a framework of fiction.

It would be misleading, however, to suggest that Eliade is the preponderant influence on Fuentes. The fact is, as Fuentes himself repeatedly points out, that the sources of influence on his work are innumerable. He does not believe "that he who reads Proust proustitutes himself," as he points out in the letter of 8 December

1968 included in the Appendix. Certainly as important as that of Eliade is the influence of Octavio Paz. And by coincidence, perhaps, both Paz and Eliade are well versed in Jungian psychology. In the case of Eliade, this influence is obvious in his frequent references to C.G. Jung. In the case of Paz, the influence is surmised because of the striking parallels in their work which Richard Callan points out in an article in *Hispania* (60 [1977] 916–26): "Some Parallels between Octavio Paz and Carl Jung."

Thus, although we may postpone for the moment the question of whether Fuentes is himself directly or indirectly influenced by Jungian psychology, there is no question that Jung is fundamental for any modern investigation, anthropological, psychological or literary, into the subject of myth. It is Jung who has given myth a semi-scientific respectability, fused anthropology, religion, abnormal psychology and literature into an interrelated whole. The study of Fuentes as literary creator of myth must, therefore, begin with a study of the dream figures that led Freud's onetime follower to elaborate this theory of myth and the collective unconscious.

Jung believed that myths were constructed upon *archetypal figures* which he emphasized were "forms or images of a collective nature which occur practically all over the earth at the same time as autochtonous individual products of unconscious origin."[6] These archetypal figures would include the witch figure or the virgin mother figure, both of which seem to be particular manifestations of a more inclusive archetype, which he calls the anima. It is only through the insight provided by the works of Jung, for example, that we can explain why the witch figure in both literature and history is predominantly a feminine one. (The new scholastic organization WITCH, we must remember, is a women's club.) The largely historical approaches to the study of witchcraft seem at a loss, on the whole, to provide a conclusive explanation for the witch's femaleness. For example, Hill and Williams, in *The Supernatural*, assert that

> women have always predominated in the history of witches, and a host of more or less unsatisfactory explanations of this fact could be cited. For instance, 16th Century writers felt that women were more credulous and impressionable than men, and so more easily tempted by Satan. Others felt that Satan, being a male personification of evil, preferred women assistants. Later authorities, like the 19th Century French pathologist J. M. Charcot, saw that demonic possession was in fact a form of hysteria (from *hyster,* the Greek word for uterus). They considered it primarily a female sexual disorder. Anthropologists, recalling the female shamans of many primitive tribes, suggested that the supposedly 'irrational' tendencies of the female left an opening for occult and quasi-religious belief. Probably the real explanation (if there is one) will somehow be connected with the fact that women were for so long thought to be inferior beings and thus were considered more susceptible to foolishness and sin. . . .[7]

Historical explanations, therefore, as the authors themselves admit, are unsatisfactory. As I have indicated, the only satisfactory explanation for the femaleness of the witch is the one provided by Jung in his numerous studies related to the anima.[8]

Jung's Theory of the Anima

Jung's theory, which is both physiological and psychological, might be summarized as follows: a person's sex is determined by the preponderance of male- or female-producing genes in the combined chromosomes of sperm and ovum after fertilization. Biologically a man contains female-producing elements, a woman male-producing ones, elements which are latent in his or her personality. The trained psychiatrist can discover astonishing symptoms of the man in the woman, and vice versa. This "other side," a woman in man and a man in woman, he has called the "anima" and "animus" respectively. The anima causes illogical moods and the animus produces unreasonable opinions.[9]

In Jung's words:

> If we compare a number of emotional events, we see that the same character reappears in every one of them. For this reason we attribute continuity to the unconscious personality. . . . Patients often suffer so much from the intrusion of the unconscious that it helps them to know their opponent personally. The anima sometimes appears personified in dreams and other products of unconscious activity. We also find her as a classical figure in prose fiction. Always there is an element of the supernatural adhering to the anima. Her moral range is wide. She embraces the degraded woman and the *femme inspiratrice*. She has given rise to the mythological goddess.[10]

In a later study with Kerényi, Jung identifies the anima even further:

> In the products of unconscious activity the anima appears equally as maiden and mother. . . . She is bipolar and can therefore appear positive one moment and negative the next; now maiden, now a good fairy, now a witch. Besides this ambivalence, the anima also has occult connections with the world

of darkness in general and for that reason is often of a religious complexion. Whenever she emerges with some degree of clarity, she always has a peculiar relationship to time; as a rule she is more or less immortal because outside time.[11]

The witch for Jung, therefore, is a female product of the male unconscious which can appear in myths, fairy tales, dreams, and products of psychotic fantasy.[12] She appears as "the individual property of each one of us" as in dreams and yet, "even dreams are made up of collective material to a very high degree."[13] Archetypal motifs such as the witch presumably start from patterns of the human mind and are not only transmitted by tradition and migration, but also by heredity. This latter hypothesis, Jung has stated, "is indispensable since even complicated archetypal images can be spontaneously reproduced without any possible direct tradition."[14]

The foregoing quotations and summaries of Jung are included for the reader to gain some clue, some insight into the fascination of the witch for Carlos Fuentes. I have not depended upon Jung, I should point out, because of any direct influence by Jung on Fuentes's work. The very fact that Fuentes at one time confessed himself to be totally unacquainted with Jung (see the letter of 24 July 1969 in the Appendix) is an example in itself of the totally unconscious nature of the archetypal figures which may appear to any one of us in dreams, or be faithfully reproduced by the writer who is unfamiliar with their Jungian classifications. As Fuentes remarks in the letter cited above, "My intuition of the mythical must be a priori."

Yet we must consider the possibility, of course, that through scholars such as Paz, Eliade, or Lévi-Strauss, Jung's ideas have found their way to Fuentes. This possibility Fuentes also points out in the above mentioned letter. He says, "a posteriori, any ideas I now have about

the subject [myth] are very much due to Lévi-Strauss;
the myth as a perpetual present, the myth as itself plus
all the commentaries it has provoked, myth as a chain
of reflection, myth as the oldest form of social discourse
between body and soul, living and dead, remembered
and foreseen, etc.''

But these ideas that Fuentes mentions are of a general,
highly theoretical nature. Although he seems to deny
the Jungian concept of a collective unconscious, Lévi-
Strauss nevertheless speaks of an innate myth-making
process in mankind. Thus although Lévi-Strauss does
not to my knowledge deal with Jung's specific archetypal
figures, only referring to them in the vaguest of terms,[15]
they are nevertheless to be found in Fuentes's works
with surprising frequency and coinciding in many details with the Jungian figures drawn from the realm of
fairy tales, dreams, and religious mythology. This spontaneous appearance of the archetypes in Fuentes only
seems to confirm Jung's idea of a collective unconscious
in its aspect of inheritable preconceptions.

I shall rely on Jung, therefore, not because of any direct influence that he has had on Fuentes, but rather as
a tool for understanding all archetypal literature, an approach that even so hostile a critic of the psychological
attitude applied to literature as Northrop Frye grants is
sometimes valid.[16] I see no reason why we should not
avail ourselves of the clues provided by Jung's anima,
and his other archetypal figures such as the Great
Mother, to understand better not only Fuentes's *Aura*,
for example, but the works of such pre-Jungian writers
as Alexander Pushkin and Henry James. Once we grant
that the archetypal image as a product of the collective
unconscious is created spontaneously by writers of different nationalities and of different historical periods,
the problem of "literary" influence in similar works, as
we shall see in our study of *Aura*, becomes unimportant.

However, it would be misleading to suggest that

Fuentes's ideas coincide with Jung's interpretation of
the collective unconscious in all respects. In the case of
Fuentes there is a strong dose of Freudian psychology
and a tendency to view the unconscious from the more
negative viewpoint of Freud than that of Jung, who ascribed positive as well as negative attributes to it.[17] This
instinctively negative reaction to the unconscious by
Fuentes is seen clearly in his allusion (see the 8 December letter in the Appendix) to the mass killing of
students "in the ill-named 'Square of the Three Cultures'" as a resurgence of the "collective subconscious."[18] For Jung, on the other hand, this phenomenon
would be called a "collective seizure" to which modern
man and mobs are prey.[19] The term "collective unconscious," (rather than "subconscious" with its suggestion
of inferiority) is used instead to indicate the collective
substratum of the personal unconscious, the matrix of
the archetypal figures.[20]

Thus, although the attitude of Fuentes with respect
to the collective unconscious differs from that of Jung,
his use of the archetypal figures indicates an implicit
acceptance of this zone in the human psyche which was
largely ignored by Freud. For this reason, whatever
Fuentes's personal sympathies, a Freudian analysis of
his works would tend to involve biographical material
about him to a far greater extent than is necessary or
useful, and would reduce the witch figure to his erotic
suppressed fears or longings (specifically the well-known
Oedipus complex), an interpretation as simple as it is
misleading. Although Fuentes, like Freud, gives tremendous importance to sex in his works, unlike Freud,
Fuentes is prone to use sex for metaphysical reasons.
(In Freud, we may recall, the sexual urge is to be expressed leaving the individual free to pursue his posi-
tivistic goals. In Fuentes, as we shall see in our study
of *Aura* and *Holy Place*, the sexual act in fact serves as

a ritual connection with the universe. Ironically, therefore, it is both more and less important than in Freud.)

The Witch and Social Reform

In speaking of Freud, it is perhaps interesting to note
that in his early work he mistrusted artistic therapy and
believed that through art the artist escaped reality and
found substitute gratifications. However, in later years
he moderated this attitude, coming closer to Lionel Trilling who has stated that art can shape one's fantasies and
give them social form and reference.[21] This problem of
the relationship of art to society is one that has troubled
not only Freud, Trilling, Nietzsche, and a host of others
(including Jung, who questioned, like Nietzsche, whether
the artist had the physical time or energy to develop
himself as a complete individual and also fulfill his artistic mission),[22] but also Fuentes.

There is an apparent dichotomy in Fuentes's position
as an ardent advocate of the left in all his public utter-
ances, and his artistic concern with a nonrealistic genre,
especially in his latest novels. The problem emerges:
how does Fuentes reconcile his interest in witches and
magic with his concern for social reform?

His first step, I would say, is to deny the problem. He
does this by rejecting the doctrine of socialist realism
which, literally interpreted, would require that an artist's
work must have an easily recognizable political complexion. Instead, as in the declaration of Latin American
writers published in Havana in 1966 and signed by
Fuentes, he would assign a dual task to the writer: "to
participate as an intellectual in the struggle for basic
change in Latin America, and as an artist to remain responsible to his art by whatever techniques and approaches to reality which will serve his creative aims."[23]

But more than this, Fuentes seems to see his roles as an intellectual and an artist as complementary. As an artist he chooses fantasy and parody in order to magnify the demonic element in bourgeois society and so help prepare its inevitable (from a Marxian viewpoint) collapse. Yet the relevance of artistic expression to social communication in Fuentes is not always as clear for the reader as Fuentes might suppose. There are moments when the artist seems to contradict the social reformer, when humanity's fate is so inexorably determined by demonic forces in control of the universe that any political solution becomes vapid and irrelevant. And yet according to one branch of the modern Freudian school represented by Franz Alexander, this dilemma of the artist is today inevitable. Alexander wrote in 1953:

> The naked unconscious as it often appears in contemporary art is not a suitable way of communication. It must go through the prism of the organizing portion of the personality, the conscious ego, in order to become meaningful. The artist eventually will emerge from the surrealistic detour through the depths of the unconscious with a new constructive message which he cannot express in this era of doubt and confusion.[24]

This negative influence of society upon the possibilities of artistic creation is echoed by one of Fuentes's characters, a painter, in the short story from *Cantar de ciegos (Song of the Blind)*, 1964, "Fortuna lo que ha querido" ("What Chance Has Wished"):

> Before I wished to say that among ourselves a sacred art was possible. All my figures were a representation of the dark side and the sacred which continued to exist in our total being. . . . Art needs

a heaven and an inferno, an extreme possibility beyond the earth.

Now neither the earth nor man are sacred. This
is what is sacred. This final profanity. This thing that
I give them. Not fine sentiments, nor the human
figure, nor liberated matter, nor light nor a pure
rhombus. No. Here is the only thing that is sacred,
the negation of the sacred. What *they* use. (3d ed.
[Mexico, D.F.: Joaquín Mortiz, 1967], p. 62)

By *they*, Fuentes of course refers to society since the
protagonist is justifying his role as a pop artist who has
just painted a huge jar of Nestlé's instant coffee. Pop art
is justified as an abomination *in a period that demands
abominations,* and here we may suspect that Fuentes is
speaking in his own defense since there is a strong element of pop art in his novels. He readily confessed this
in his already cited interview with Rodríguez-Monegal,
claiming that "In this novel [*Change of Skin*] there is
a kind of indiscrimination that is typical of the attitude
of pop."[25] There is also much of the spirit of pop art in
Holy Place which, like *Change of Skin,* is based on the
movies in that it depicts the life of a kind of actress only
the movie industry could have created. Both works, like
the movies of the thirties which serve Fuentes as a point
of reference, are permeated by the spirit of parody, and
portray a world of false values that sometimes reaches
the state of fantasy.

The Literary Approach to Demonic Art

The current interest by Fuentes in fantasy and parody
is typical of what a myth-oriented literary critic, Northrop Frye, considers to be the literary phase that accom-
panies "the collapse and disintegration of the comic so-

ciety." It is marked by "works such as ghost stories, thrillers and Gothic romances, and on a more sophisticated level, [by] the kind of imaginative withdrawal portrayed by Huysman's *À Rebours.*" Frye explains: "The comic society has run the full course from infancy to death, and in its last phase myths closely connected psychologically with a return to the womb are appropriate."[26]

It is curious to see how the latest works of Fuentes, which at first sight appear so experimental, so revolutionary in technique, do contain many of the elements enumerated by Frye as typical of the "final stage of comedy" (a stage that is literary, but has strong sociological overtones). Like Huysman's Des Esseintes, the narrator of *Change of Skin,* for example, may be considered "a dilettante trying to amuse himself."[27] But if the term "comedy" seems a little inappropriate in view of Fuentes's basically tragic philosophy, perhaps the more popular expression "black humor" will make the classification clearer. In *Aura,* for example, a young man goes to bed with someone he imagines to be a beautiful girl and wakes up with an old, wrinkled woman (who also happens to be a witch); in *Holy Place,* the beautiful mother punishes her naughty son by turning him into a dog. The tragic element always has humorous overtones. Frye's last stage of comedy is one totally invaded by parodic and ironic elements, dominated by an attitude of satire. Fuentes's later novels have their share of verbal tempests ("I am a putter-inner, not a taker-outer," Fuentes says in his interview with Rodríguez-Monegal), and the erudite technicalities that we find in Joyce, and especially the use of parodic religious symbols suggesting some form of Satan- or AntiChrist-worship.[28]

Thus we see that Fuentes's concern with witches and the world of parody and fantasy is a typical literary reaction to a given set of social circumstances. It is only by bearing in mind the historical, psychological, and social background of the witches (and other archetypal characters) as they appear in Fuentes's work, that we may fully appreciate their significance. As I treat them now in greater detail, I shall sometimes use one approach, sometimes another—whichever seems to provide the more incisive tool. They are all, I believe, valid perspectives on a fascinating and often elusive subject.

II
Aura and its Precedents in Fuentes's Earlier Works

Aura: The Plot

Aura is a fairy tale for adults set in the enchanted land of Mexico City today. The hero, Felipe Montero, is a young historian who answers a newspaper advertisement which he feels is directed specifically to him. He finds himself in the shadowy, old mansion of an indescribably ancient woman, Consuelo Llorente. Immediately Felipe is hired to edit the memoirs of Consuelo's husband, the dead General Llorente, and is introduced to Consuelo's niece, Aura, a beautiful young girl of twenty. These are the only human inhabitants of the mansion. The others are animals, either seen or heard— a huge rabbit, the pet of Consuelo, and the cats and rodents whose presence is made known to the hero only by their sounds.

In the swiftly moving story, Felipe falls in love with Aura at first sight and before the next night has passed, she comes of her own accord to share his bed. Yet to his dismay he soon realizes that Aura is more automaton than woman, that her very motions echo those of her aunt. And he at first imagines that she is held prisoner by the old woman.

But little by little the general's memoirs reveal the

truth of the matter. Consuelo, in her desperate longing
to have a child, had resorted to herbs and magic until
she could create a child of the spirit if not of the flesh.
In some way, Felipe realizes, Aura is a creation of the
"aunt." And she is an imperfect creation. When he sees
Aura again only one day has passed, yet she has aged by
twenty years. But his love for her has not diminished.
The study of the memoirs, especially the photographs
of the dead general and the young Consuelo, gradually
lead him to an even more amazing revelation. *He* is in
fact the general reincarnated, and Aura is the young Consuelo. In his last night with Aura the mask of youth of
the widow is stripped off completely as moonlight reveals her again as a wrinkled hag. She can only summon
forth the form of Aura for three days, she confesses. This
is the limit of her powers. But with Felipe's help, they
will try again to bring back the image of her lost youth.

The Archetypal Pattern

If we reduce *Aura* to its basic components—old witch,
beautiful young girl who is a ward of the witch, young
stranger who falls victim to the old woman, crumbling
mansion as setting—we see that the pattern is duplicated
in a number of works of literature with only slight variations. Perhaps most notable are Pushkin's *Queen of
Spades*, and *The Aspern Papers* by Henry James. But
whereas in the case of Fuentes one may point to the
influence of the earlier works with which Fuentes, in
his letter of 8 December 1968, confesses a familiarity,
in the case of James it is impossible to prove any knowledge of the work by Pushkin.[1] Yet, as I have indicated
in an earlier study,[2] the coincidence between these
works is not unusual.

Jung has told us that when dealing with archetypal

characters and their attendant myths, the risk of dupli-
cation is always present. Pierre Benoit, for example, was
accused of plagarizing H. Rider Haggard "because the
accounts of the heroine in Haggard's *Wisdom's Daughter*
and Benoit's *L'Atlantide* were disconcertingly alike."[3]
This is true because in dealing with fantasies of this
kind, the details of character are insignificant. Such stories do not deal with individuals as such, but rather with
overwhelming forces in the human psyche which are
essentially the same in everyone. Their inspiration is
philosophical or religious and has little to do with the
vagaries of individual personality. Thus Joseph Sommers has stated: "A fair general statement would be that
the conceptual basis of *Aura* is rooted in the eternal
mysteries which overcome man." Although he does not
mention Pushkin, he traces the work's literary paternity
to Edgar Allan Poe and the English gothic novel, and
asserts that "despite the indirect vision it projects of the
Mexican experience, [it] is more suggestive of European
and American heritage than of its Mexican forebears.[4]
Fuentes himself in his letter of December 1968 also cites
influences in *Aura* from other Latin American novelists,
notably José Donoso's *Coronación* (which is also based
on the archetypal pattern of the young and old female
inhabitants of a mansion).

The fact is that *Aura* is a comment about life, about
man's destiny and not about what happened to an individual, Felipe Montero. In an interview with Fuentes,
Sommers contrasts this work to *The Death of Artemio
Cruz* where man, who is capable of rational choice, de-
termines his own destiny. *Aura*, according to Sommers,
is the other face of the coin, where "the blind side of
man is portrayed; he is a prisoner of the occult forces of
irreality, phantasy and myth." Fuentes concurs in this
analysis and adds that in *The Death of Artemio Cruz* he
had relied on the illumination of historical analysis. In

Aura, he depended upon "the multilayered suggestivity of literary style."[5]

I might add that the two conflicting elements of Fuentes's earliest novel, *Where the Air is Clear*, the realistic development of character and rational political commentary (the major emphasis) and the minor note of magic and fatalism—to be discussed later in this chapter—are finally isolated in these two separate novels, both published in 1962. *The Death of Artemio Cruz* carries the major theme in its concern with the Mexican revolution and its development of the character, Artemio Cruz, out of his prototype in Federico Robles. *Aura* carries out the other theme of modern Mexico born out of the ancient one and returning to it, a theme first interpreted by Emir Rodríguez-Monegal in an article in *Número* ("El mundo mágico de Carlos Fuentes," *Número*, 2d ser. 1 [1963]:144–59), which appeared a scant year after the publication of *Aura*.

Los Dias Enmascarados

In the discussion of *Aura* I shall need to refer to all of its precedents, not only Fuentes's major, first novel, but also his earlier book of short stories, *Los dias enmascarados* (*The Masked Days*), first published in 1952. We may judge the similarity of this work to *Aura* by the commentary of Robert Mead, Jr.: "*Los dias enmascarados* is in the cosmopolitan vein of Jorge Luis Borges, and is written for sophisticated readers. Life is a comedy played against a serious and somber background, in which the author presents man as struggling unsuccessfully against forces far stronger than himself."[6]

In one of these stories, "Tlactocatzine, del Jardín de Flandes," the similarities with *Aura* are striking. The story, too, is a tale of an old mansion in Mexico City with a mysterious garden. Told in the first person, it narrates the hero's encounters with an intruder, a wrinkled hag in historical costume. Like the garden in *Aura* where strange, medicinal herbs are grown, this one is permeated by the odor of *Siemprevivas,* (literally "alive-forever," the Spanish for forget-me-nots).

The hag or witch, by means of letters, invites the narrator to a midnight tryst in the garden where he feels in her hands the coldness of the tomb. He tries to escape the mansion, but finds the door locked against him. The hag now calls him "Max" as well as "Tlactocatzine," speaks German as well as Nahuatl, and reminds him of their walks in the garden of Flanders. When he examines the shield on the locked door, he perceives a crowned eagle that seems to have the profile of the old woman. The suspicion with respect to her identity is confirmed when he reads the inscription on the shield, "Charlotte, Kaiserin von Mexico."

To summarize, therefore, we have in this story an atmosphere of increasing unreality. The mansion, which at first is merely beautiful and archaic, actually could exist in Mexico City. But when we discover that it rains always in the garden when the sun is shining in the outside world, we are put on guard. The tale becomes increasingly less real and more subjective. The creature who inhabits the garden is merely hinted at in the first reference: "one might almost say that slow steps are heard with the weight of breath among the fallen leaves."[7]

But gradually, she grows to a certainty. At the conclusion her personality invades the entire house and imprisons the narrator forever. There is no escape from this symbol of the past who seems to be part Aztec princess and part Charlotte, wife of the emperor Maximilian. The latter figure is superimposed on the former. In a way, Charlotte is almost as much a prisoner of the earlier primitive archetype as is the narrator. She too has been caught by history and in turn must prey on others, must find new Maximilians, new victims. For the narrator she embodies "the satisfaction of the jailer, of eternal prison, satisfaction of shared solitudes" (p. 50).

The probability that "Tlactocatzine," which we know was written together with the other stories of the collection "in some haste" as reported by Luis Harss and Barbara Dohmann (*Into the Mainstream* [New York: Harper and Row, 1967], p. 284), was in fact the rough draft for *Aura* is suggested by the December letter from Fuentes (included in the Appendix) in which he discusses the germinal idea for the novel.

After enumerating the long line of witches who appear in his works from "Tlactocatzine" to "the old Ludivinia, shut up in the only room of a burned down mansion in *The Death of Artemio Cruz*, he adds:

> But if I am totally frank, this obsession was born in me when I was seven years old and, after visiting the castle of Chapultepec and seeing the portrait of the young Charlotte of Belgium, I found in the Casasola Archive the photograph of this same woman, now old, dead, placed inside her cushioned, iron coffin, dressed in the nightcap of a little girl; the Charlotte who died, insane in a castle the same year I was born. The two Charlottes, Aura and Consuelo. Perhaps Charlotte never found out that she was growing old. Until the very end she wrote love letters to Maximillian. A correspondence between ghosts.[8]

The empress Carlota (Charlotte) is clearly the inspiration for both these tales. And how well she conforms to the idea of the anima! She is youth and age (since

Fuentes sees her image at both extremes of life); as an empress she represents power; and as a woman insane she is the perfect symbol of our irrational, hidden nature. For Fuentes as a Mexican, moreover, Carlota would represent the European domination of the past, and would thus repel him. Yet as a beautiful and tragic woman, she could not help but also attract a sensitive child of cosmopolitan background.

Jung has told us that the first manifestation of archetypes is often identified with personal experience; that in the case of archetypes in children under the influence of therapy, "the identity breaks down and is accompanied by intensification of the fantasy, with the result that the archaic or mythological features become increasingly apparent."[9]

This obviously is the case history of Carlota in her metamorphosis in Fuentes's mind from portrait to ghost. His brief commentary on the role of Carlota, "correspondence between ghosts," indicates his very subjective relationship to the archetypal character. In Fuentes's mind Carlota is already a ghost corresponding with the "real" ghost of her husband. In "Tlactocatzine" Charlotte is even aware, momentarily, that hers is a correspondence between ghosts: "Ah, Max, answer me, the forget-me-nots that I take you in the afternoon to the Capuchin crypt, don't they smell fresh?" (p. 50).

Again, in commenting on *Aura* to Harss and Dohmann, Fuentes uses the same word, *fantasma*, ghost. "Every story is written with a ghost at your shoulder." In *Aura* the ghost is Woman.[10] What does the word *ghost* mean or suggest to Fuentes, that he repeatedly applies it to the archetypal figure of Carlota-Aura? It has, of course, many connotations, but perhaps chief among them are death, the past, and the supernatural, ideas which are also associated with the anima.

But the use of the word *ghost* is unfortunate in that
Harss and Dohmann then proceed to judge *Aura* as a
ghost story, a genre whose requirements of suspense it
fails to fulfill. "For a meaning to be revealed," they say,
"it must first be withheld."[11] One of the problems with
Aura seems to be that the "ghost" is too close to the
archetypal figure, and although the meaning may not be
"handed out," as the critics charge, it is suspected by
the reader from the beginning.

The Themes in *Aura*

The problem at hand, therefore, is why Fuentes, with
all his literary dexterity, uses in *Aura* (and elsewhere)
an undisguised archetypal figure which is so vulnerable
to criticism. I would postulate that at least part of the
reason lies in his didacticism. Since the significance of
the archetypal figure is more obvious than that of a character complicated by an involved personal history,
Fuentes, when he wishes to be sure of making a point,
utilizes the former as a kind of literary shorthand. And
this point, to which he sacrifices character development,
is usually of a philosophical or social nature. If this postulation is correct, I am in opposition to Robert Mead,
who, in commenting upon *Los dias enmascarados,* asserts that "absent from it is the intense preoccupation
with social problems which characterize most of his later
work."[12]

In support of my interpretation of the motivation behind Fuentes's less realistic fiction is a statement Fuentes
made to Sommers: "*Aura*, despite its basis in a highly
subjective, even phantasmagoric view of reality, ultimately implies and reveals an external world."[13] The fact
that many of Fuentes's works do not reflect the external

world as we know it does not indicate, therefore, (as mentioned in the preceding chapter) that they are not concerned with reality or with social problems. Even Harss and Dohmann recognized that *Aura* was intended as a parable (as well as a ghost story). And Emir Rodríguez-Monegal in the already referred to article from *Número*, found that *Aura* symbolized "the reconstruction of the Mexico of the old days of privilege upon the structure of today's modern and insolent Mexico."[14]

This theme of the old built upon the new, the old returning to haunt the new, is again the theme of ghosts. And although *Aura* may not be a good ghost story, it is, I believe, intended as very much more than a mere ghost story. External reality, as in the case of "Tlactocatzine," gradually withers away. But the attempt is not so much to shock, as to make the reader more fully aware of only half-suspected truths.

The Problem of Reality: Conscious Versus Unconscious. Our first intimation that *Aura* will not deal with the recognizable world of Mexico City in 1962 is provided by the narrator's observation that the house in question is located in the old center of the city! "You always thought that nobody lived in the old center of the city" (p. 6).[15]

Thus he discovers that the past lives on, generally unnoticed, in the heart of the city—and by implication, in the hearts of its inhabitants. The theme of superimposition of personalities and cultures is also foreshadowed by Felipe's discovery that in this old *barrio* house numbers have been changed many times, new ones superimposed on the old which are nevertheless still visible.

The normal world of today begins to fade rapidly as he relates:

before going in you take a last look over your shoulder, frowning at the long line of stalled buses and cars that groan, honk and pour forth the crazy smoke of their haste. You try, uselessly, to retain a single image of this outside indifferentiated world. (p. 7).

The last adjective, "indifferentiated," suggests the fuzziness, the unreality of the normal, daylight world Felipe has left to enter the real, but shadowy, one of the old mansion. Once inside its portals, the borderline between real life and the world of dreams becomes increasingly tenuous. According to Robert Mead, "the reader ends by thinking that the entire story, from beginning to end, is a long dream, a chain of events which are born, live and die in the imagination of Felipe Montero."[16]

But the problem is not dream versus reality, but dream versus consciousness. Felipe in this dream world is learning truths to which the daylight world of the conscious ego may blind us. Thus the theme of *La vida es sueño* (*Life Is a Dream*) is clearly echoed in *Aura;* we learn from our dreams, and dreams themselves reveal an often hidden and fundamental part of reality. But there is a significant difference in the basic assumptions of Calderón and of Fuentes. In the great drama of the Golden Age life may be a dream, but the consequences of man's behavior in his dream are awesome. It is a dream dreamed in order to allocate to each of us our final place in eternity, whether this be paradise or eternal condemnation. It is a dream which is a vestibule to a permanent reality. Thus Calderón's conception of the dream is predicated on free will and personal responsibility. There is an imperative need to act wisely and generously in the knowledge that one is being judged.

But if life becomes merely a dream, as in *Aura*, if there is no hereafter of an extra-worldly nature, but only a perpetual reincarnation in this dream world (a theme to

be discussed shortly), there is no need to assume free
will. In fact the idea suggested by the word *dream* is
diametrically opposed, for the modern mind, to the ideas
of free will and individual responsibility. If something
is only a dream, we are not responsible for our actions—
which are viewed as the automatic product of our unconscious. In dreams the course of events often seems
predetermined, therefore, with little place for the dreamer's personal choice. Thus *Aura* is far closer to the dream
as we know it than is *La vida es sueño*.

There is a shadow of fate, of inevitability, of nightmare
at times rather than dream, in *Aura* from beginning to
end. In the third sentence of the novel, we read that the
newspaper advertisement that sends the hero to the old
mansion "seems directed to you and only you" (p. 9).

The Matter of Fate. The narrator walks into the trap
which is first baited by money (his need for the salary
of nine hundred pesos) and secondly by Aura, whose
green eyes enchant him immediately. He says to himself: "Don't fool yourself; these eyes flow, they are transformed, as if they were offering you a landscape that
only you could guess or desire. Yes, I am going to live
with you" (p. 15).

Then the trap is sprung. Felipe understands that "this
house will always be in darkness" (p. 21). He hears the
plaintive cries of the cats, whose very existence, as well
as that of the garden where drug-producing plants are
grown, the old woman denies; he surprises Consuelo
muttering secret words before her altar with its picture
of hell, and still he does not seem to react. He is apparently overwhelmed by curiosity as well as infatuation.
In the last scene we may recall that Felipe is in bed with
the old hag and makes no attempt to escape. Yet by this
time all illusion of beauty is gone. Nevertheless, he embraces her: "You plunge your face, your open eyes, into

Consuelo's silver-white hair, and Consuelo will embrace you again when the moon is out of sight. (p.74).[17]

The Role of Love in Aura. We have already seen in the discussion of the anima that this archetype always carries a suggestion of fate, of inevitability. In *Aura,* she draws Felipe to her home and, in part through her incarnation of Aura, keeps him there. He is troubled by attraction to Aura and on the conscious level rationalizes and tells himself that he really wishes to rescue her from the spell of the old woman. But on the unconscious level he understands that his real motive for remaining is his need for Aura.

Felipe, we must remember, is a modern man, a rootless intellectual who lives in the "labyrinth of solitude" that Octavio Paz describes, where each man is keenly aware of his isolation from other individuals. In Paz's chapter entitled "The Dialectic of Solitude" he states:

> What we ask of love (which, being desire, is a hunger for communion, a will to fall and to die as well as to be reborn) is that it give us a bit of true life, of true death. We do not ask it for happiness or repose, but simply for an instant of that full life in which opposites vanish, in which life and death, time and eternity are united. . . . Creation and destruction become one in the act of love, and during a fraction of a second man has a glimpse of a more perfect state of being.[18]

Such a penetrating analysis of love by a writer who has had a profound influence on Fuentes[19] does much to explain the pull of fate on Felipe Montero.

For Felipe, Aura symbolizes the therapy of love, a

fusion with someone outside himself. And since his desire is in itself part of the masochistic desire for self-destruction (also studied by both Freud and Jung), the "desire to fall and to die" of which Paz speaks, the dual figure of Aura-Consuelo satisfies both sides of Felipe's craving. Paz has also called this "hunger for communion," and the religious aspect of the sexual act is underlined by Fuentes. Aura's bedroom becomes a church in metaphor: "And you enter this empty bedroom where a circle of light illuminates the bed, the huge Mexican crucifix . . ."(p. 53).

And again:

> You fall on Aura's nude body, on her open arms, stretched out from one end to the other of the bed, like the black Christ that hangs from the wall with his scarlet silk wrapped around his thighs, his knees open, his wounded side, his crown of thorns set up on a tangled black wig with silver spangles. Aura opens up like an altar (p. 56).

Sommers, too, points out the black Christ and the analogy between sexual intercourse and Christian communion. Aura even places on her thighs a thin wheat biscuit suggestive of the holy wafer. Summarizing this scene, Sommers comments:

> Blacks arts, expressed in distorted religious symbols, generate a power superior to that of the intellect . . . The stature of man is diminished for he commands no resources to cope with the mysterious forces which intrude on his consciousness and on his life.[20]

Yet the stature of man does not seem to be relevant in *Aura*. Felipe is not concerned about stature. Like Paz's lonely Mexican, he is concerned about reality and real existence, and his one way of achieving this is by fusion with something outside himself.

This fusion in the minds of today's young students is found in sex and religion. That this is the key to meaning in life is also mentioned by Father Greeley. He quotes one student as saying: "The only place where we are going to find ourselves is in deep relationships with others and that means either religion or sex and maybe both."[21] Father Greeley comments:

> The religious experience in the final analysis is seen as 'ecstatic,' that is to say, that it, like sex, takes a person out of himself and brings him into contact not only with other human beings but with the 'creative powers' which presumably underpin the cosmos.[22]

But if Sommers emphasizes the negative aspect of Felipe's religious and sexual experience, it is only natural in that Fuentes himself has laden it with many of the nineteenth-century, romantic symbols of the Black Mass, the description of the wafer, the black Christ, etc. As a demonologist, he has not, in fact, clearly defined the nature of Consuelo's powers and thus has confused the moral significance of Felipe's love relationship with her. Talking to Harss and Dohmann, Fuentes seems to equate Consuelo with the ghost of Woman, "the keeper of secret knowledge, which is true knowledge, general knowledge, universal knowledge."[23] And yet, Consuelo, as we have seen, acts very much like a fairy tale witch with her casting of spells and her sacrifice of cats. There are even innuendos that through black magic she is casting an evil spell on Felipe:

> You eat mechanically, with the doll in your hand . . . without realizing, at first, your own hypnotized at-

titude, only later glimpsing a reason for your oppressive nap, your nightmare, finally identifying your somnambulist movements with those of Aura, with those of the old woman: staring with disgust at this horrid little doll that your fingers caress, where you begin to suspect there may be a secret sickness, a contagion (p. 51).

Thus Consuelo uses effigies for magic purposes; also the presence of the rabbit Saga (sagacious?) strongly suggests the familiar or witch's assistant, whose historic function has been to focus the witch's power.[24] There is also the implication that Consuelo has fallen into the sin of rebelling against God. General Llorente, in his memoirs, writes: "Consuelo, don't tempt God . . . the devil was once also an angel" (p. 69).

Does all this indicate that Consuelo is in fact a witch? And if so, what would this signify with respect to the spiritual development of Felipe?

A Definition of the Witch. This question can only be answered by recourse to a stricter definition of the term *witch* than I have hitherto provided. According to Hill and Williams, authors of *The Supernatural*, the term should really be applied only to a very limited group of individuals. As they understand the term, even if Consuelo had sold her soul to the Devil by means of a pact, she would still not necessarily be a witch. Rather she seems to belong to the ancient tradition of sorceresses "who may cast spells, charms, and hexes and stir up love potions." "Providing his end is selfish . . . that the sorcerer's motive is to gain riches, power or pleasure for himself, in this world," he is sorcerer and not witch.[25]

Such sorcerers, they say, are pagan, not anti-Christian, and were in fact critically regarded by the church as private practitioners of magic, but not seriously persecuted until the mid-fifteenth century.[26]

In order to distinguish between these suspicious but not really demonic women and real witches, Hill and Williams use the yardstick of intent. The real witch was an agent of the devil, "not one of his customers, used her magic to serve the devil's own purposes, not her own. . . . Her principal function was the worship of the devil, which involved the conscious repudiation of God and the Christian faith.[27]

One of the sources of confusion as to the love ritual in *Aura* seems to be that sex also played a fundamental role in all witch ceremonies, as did various involved perversions and obscenities. But this was pure sex, often grotesque, with no question of love. We need only read accounts of witches' covens and black masses[28] to see how radically different they were from anything found in *Aura*. (Fuentes confuses the picture by his references to the desecration of the Host and the Black Christ— elements of the Black Mass, which according to many authorities is virtually a literary creation and did not grow directly out of the tradition of witchcraft.)[29] Like all sorceresses, therefore, Consuelo uses magic for her own selfish purposes, in this case to reincarnate her youth and thereby recreate love. Richard Callan compares her to the Greek fertility goddess, Hecate, mother of witchcraft who had as her symbols dogs, goats, mice, and torches—all the items we find in the cavelike abode of Consuelo.[30] Rather than exacting Felipe's soul, she gives him a new one, or rather reveals through her love his true soul and his true face which also had belonged to her husband, the general.

The Theme of Personal Identity. Harss and Dohmann attribute *Aura*'s popularity with its author to its frontal attack on the theme of personal identity.[31] As we see in Felipe's metamorphosis, this attack certainly exists. But it is an attack that denies the problem rather than wrestling with it. Felipe, when he understands that he is in fact the general, experiences a crisis of vanity, or initial horror that his hitherto private face is really that of someone else. "You hide your face in the pillow trying to keep the air from tearing away your features which are yours, which you want for yourself" (p. 70, 71). But he seems to accept without a struggle his psychic identity with the general, "waiting for what has to come, what you can't prevent" (p. 71).

His confidence in the rational world where I am I and not someone else is entirely gone. On one level we may know, as Professor René Dubos points out, that "the individuality of a person living now is different from that of anyone who has ever lived in the past or will live in the future," that our personalities are shaped by the peculiarities of genetic endowment and the individual response to the total environment.[32] But on the deeper, unconscious level that Felipe has entered, all this is irrelevant. Almost with relief he accepts the idea that he is the general, and speculates on the nature of time which has given him an identity out of the past.

The Nature of Time In Aura. Through spiritual and bodily fusion with Aura, Felipe has apparently experienced something positive, ineffable, which can be compared not to the Black Mass but to the Mass itself. The real Mass, if properly understood, is, in the words of Jung, "a participation in the transcendence of life which overcomes all bonds of space and time. It is a moment of eternity in time."[33]

In like manner, Paz and Father Greeley have told us, man seeks fusion in love with the outside world. And he desires not only fusion in space, but also fusion in time. The dichotomy between chronological "normal" time with its generative feeling of unreality and subjective, eternal time, Paz says, "is expressed in the oppo-

sition between history and myth, or history and poetry."[34] Love is "only an instant of real life in which the
opposites of life and death, time and eternity, fuse."[35]

The love scene between Aura and Felipe, therefore,
is dominated, as is the entire novel, not by a search for
identity but rather by a secret longing to lose our painful
identities in an eternal world of space and time outside
previous experience. In the anima, young and old,
maiden and mother, is incarnated a magical conception
of time which finally penetrates Felipe's being. Real-
izing he is now a new person, Felipe says:

> You don't look at your watch again. It is a useless
> object falsely measuring a time determined by hu-
> man vanity, these little hands that tediously measure
> off the long hours invented in order to disguise the
> real passage of time, which races with an insulting
> and mortal swiftness that no clock could measure
> (p. 71).

He seems in these words to regard himself from a vantage point outside time, a vantage point that makes normal concepts absurd: "A life, a century, fifty years, it will
no longer be possible for you to imagine such lying meas-
urements" (p. 71).

The ending of the novel is ambiguous, and although
we realize that normal concepts of time are displaced,
precisely what we are to substitute in their stead is left
to the reader's imagination. There is, of course, the possibility that Felipe is only a ghost summoned by Consuelo, much as Aura has been materialized by her; that,
like the narrator in Borges's "The Circular Ruins," he
is himself only a dream. There is also the postulation of
Richard Callan that the whole story is a "hypnagogic
drama of Felipe Montero, similar to the fantasies studied
by Jung.[36] My own feeling is that it is almost useless to

divide Fuentes's characters into "real" and "unreal" cat-
egories since they all participate equally of the world of
myth, are all outside time and inside immortality. Specifically, Felipe is a new reincarnation of a prototype
that had previously existed as General Llorente. In one
of his conversations with Aura, for example, there is talk
of death and rebirth: "You have to be reborn, Aura," he
says. And she replies, "One must die first in order to be
reborn" (p. 63). Reincarnation is also the assumption in
many other stories dealing with the anima (as for example H. Rider Haggard's *She* and Poe's "Ligeia"), and,
perhaps even more important in dealing with Fuentes,
it is also to be found in the ideas of Nietzsche.[37]

Felipe seems to know his role and to accept it fatal-
istically because it is a repetition. He has done it all
before. Thus the "tú," the second person, familiar form
in which the story is written, may be interpreted as his
older, wiser, unconscious self who is privy to the secret
of fate, who observes Felipe's movements from the vantage point of past experience. He knows precisely what
Felipe is going to do because he has already done it in
a previous existence. Thus, although the narrator speaks
frequently in the future tense, there is a strong element
of the past; it is an inevitable future.[38]

Summary of Conclusions Relating to *Aura*

On the psychological plane, therefore, the character of
Aura-Consuelo is an excellent example of Jung's anima,
the archetype of life. Aura, with her green eyes, pictured
against a green sea (the photo taken of her by General
Llorente), youthful, ancient, wise and seductive, is a
composite of life-giving symbols. Offering Felipe the
hidden powers of the unconscious as *femme inspiratrice*,
she at first spurs him on to a burst of energy in his re-

search and writing. But as Richard Callan points out, Felipe fails the challenge offered him by the anima, fails to slay the dragon of Consuelo, who represents the fatal attraction of the unconscious. Instead of reasserting his ego, Felipe Montero, whose name means *hunter*, fails the test. (Given Fuentes's fatalism, of course, this was predictable from the start.) Montero succumbs to the consolation (epitomized by Consuelo whose name means *consolation*) of the Great Mother figure. Unable to rescue the anima from the engulfing form of the great feminine unconscious, he enters the world of Aura, whose name can mean *vulture, gentle breeze, breath,* or *dawn.* But Felipe chooses the dark side of her nature and pays for his choice by loss of personal identity.[39]

On the level of historical symbolism, the theme of *Aura* implies the takeover of the new by the old, and specifically the reconquest of modern Mexico by the ghosts of her past, a theme that Fuentes had already developed in *Where the Air is Clear,* and repeats again and again. So viewed, the resemblance of Aura to the figure of witch is emphasized, and she can only be regarded negatively.

Yet the meaning of *Aura* goes beyond the parochial experience of Mexico. The roots of *Aura,* as I have pointed out, are universal. The message has an almost biblical theme. As Jung says of the anima, she "is full of snares and traps in order that man should fall, should reach the earth and entangle himself there, and stay caught, so that life should be lived."[40]

Herein lies the great danger of the anima figure. Though she is irresistible as muse and young maiden, we have seen that she has as her negative pole the all-embracing figure of the Great Mother. (The relationship between anima and the other denizens of the collective unconscious are traced in detail by Erich Neumann, one of Jung's leading disciples, in *The Great Mother* [Princeton: Princeton University Press, 1955.]) As Neumann points out, the anima stands like a beacon on the threshold of the collective unconscious, and her blinding light conceals the dark form of the elemental female who lurks behind her. In psychoanalytical terms, Felipe succumbs to the pull of the uroboric unconscious represented by Consuelo, the Great Mother, relinquishes his precious ego with hardly a struggle and slips back with relief into the original state of unconsciousness and death.

In conclusion, therefore, whether we designate Aura as witch or sorceress, it is clear that her powers are both destructive and creative. This is the reason why Fuentes's attitude to the anima figure is ambiguous. She both attracts and repels him. He feels a compulsion to repeat her image again and again, perhaps hoping that some day she can be seized and tamed. Aura is the model for a later short story, "La Muñeca Reina" ("The Queen Doll") from *Cantar de ciegos* (*Song of the Blind,* 1964), which gives a fairly realistic treatment of the deformation by time of a beautiful young girl who becomes a thing of repulsion. Still another story in the same collection, "Las Dos Elenas," has its roots in *Aura,* with its treatment of the dual attraction of the old mother-in-law and the young bride for the modern, but confused, young Mexican narrator.

Other Witches in Fuentes's Early Works

Ludivinia of The Death of Artemio Cruz. If we project our study of *Aura* not into the future but into the earlier works of Fuentes, we will also see that Aura has her precedents. "Tlactocatzine, of the garden in Flanders" was one of these. Even as he worked on *Aura,* Fuentes reminds us in his letter of 8 December 1968, he was incorporating another sorceress, "the old Ludivinia," into *The Death of Artemio Cruz*. Even this, his most realistic novel, has, therefore, its version of the archetypal character.

But the treatment of Ludivinia is basically realistic, and we recognize her for the archetypal figure that she is only by a few hints. Whereas Consuelo is at least 112 years old, Ludivinia is a respectable ninety-three. And like Consuelo, she lives in the embrace of a generous past: "She wanted to know nothing except the room and her memories."[41] And, like Consuelo again, she lives with her own image of a young bride: "Now my whole life goes with me and I don't need to be an old woman" (p. 288). Ludivinia too has the wisdom of the anima, which we might call feminine intuition: "Have you come to tell me what I have always known would happen since my first night as a wife?" (p. 287). A symbol of life, she rejoices to see her own existence prolonged in the intuited grandchild: "She had seen those green eyes and had cackled with pleasure to know that she was born again in new flesh." (p. 282).

In summary, Ludivinia merely suggests the sorceress; given the realistic framework of the novel, her magical aspect is absent. She is, moreover, a minor character who only appears at the very end of the novel. Yet in one peculiar way she foreshadows the most fully developed witch in Fuentes's pantheon of magical women. Ludivinia rejects her own son: "No one has a right to be loved without a reason. Blood ties are not reason enough." (p. 288). In this Ludivinia anticipates Claudia Nervo of *Holy Place*, the witch who in fact disposes of her son by turning him into a dog.

Where the Air Is Clear: *Teódula Moctezuma*. Some of Fuentes's earlier witches, we are told by the novelist himself, are drawn directly from life and are not dreams or imaginative projections of historical characters. Discussing *Where the Air Is Clear* in an interview, he says:

For us it is more fantastic to see a hotel of forty
stories than a sorceress. There are two sorceresses
in my novel and I have known both of them. One
was an old indian woman who was called Teódula
Moctezuma. She covered herself with incredible
jewels that no one dared steal from her. She kept
the skulls of her children which, on holidays, she
painted in blue or in white colors. In my book she
represents the nocturnal horror of Mexican sacrifices.[42]

Teódula, then, is a genuine Aztec sorceress. Though,
like Consuelo, she is associated with the anima, Teódula
is far closer to the archetype of the Terrible Mother most
perfectly incarnate in India's goddess Kali, the Mexican
Tonantzin (as Fuentes refers to her in his letter of 8
December), or the Mayan goddess, Ixchel. Like Teódula,
these goddesses (who incarnate the *vagina dentata* symbolism of the tooth- or knife-studded womb) have bones
for adornment and symbolize the female as maw, coffin,
cave, or voracious earth. In ancient Greece, the Gorgon
with her hair of serpents symbolized this negative power
of the archetypal feminine. In all cases, the Terrible
Mothers are nourished by blood sacrifice. Teódula is no
exception.

Her great occult powers require repeated sacrifices
which the partially mythical son, Ixca Cienfuegos, is
duty bound to supply in the form of defenseless women
or orphaned children. Teódula's is the voice of the earth
itself, the constant bookkeeper of human lives: "The
earth claims everything . . . claims it back, swallows
everyone, to return them to us as they ought to be, even
if dead."[43]

She is the spokeswoman of the "old-time religion" of
the Aztecs predicated on this massive human sacrifice
to maintain the cosmogeny: "Our gods walk abroad, invisible but alive. . . . They always win. They take our

sacrificed blood, our killed heroes. . . . We are coming near the parting of the waters. They will die and we will be resurrected, fed by their deaths" (p. 270). Incredibly old like all archetypal figures of the mother (she recalls that as a young woman she saw the Emperor Maximilian), Teódula paints and decorates the bones of her ancestors which she carries with her. She lives in a dream of earlier civilizations, a dream sustained by sacrifice. This sacrifice is not only *of* others. Teódula also *invites* others to join her in her rituals of death: " 'I have completed the sacrifice,' she hissed into Cienfuegos' ear. 'Now we can return to being what we are, my son' . . . The old woman extended a finger . . . toward the dawning sun. 'Look, there it rises again ' " (p. 323).

We notice that Teódula, like Tonantzin, is the modern Mexican version of Coatlicue, the Aztec goddess of creation and destruction. Her sacrifices, as we note above, are aimed at propitiating the old gods, and specifically in effecting the birth of day, the rising of the sun. Fuentes's very description of the sound of her voice, her "hissing," suggests the snake-skirted goddess always pictured in Aztec art with her necklace of severed hearts and hands.

As Tonantzin, Teódula may not really be blood mother to Ixca, but merely high priestess whom he, as a believer, is forced to obey. In a final scene, in which there is another attempted sacrifice, this one of himself and his friend Rodrigo, Ixca in fact complains bitterly of his mother: "She forced me to live with that servant girl and her children again in darkness. You don't know my mother, Rodrigo. *My mother is made of stone and of serpents*" (p. 361). (The italics here are mine.) This is obviously a reference to the huge stone statue of Coatlicue in the National Museum of Mexico. Alfonso Caso in *La Religión de los Aztecas* describes the statue as follows:

> She wears a skirt made of intertwined serpents as
> suggested in her name, and all held together by an-
> other serpent which acts as a belt. . . . Her feet and
> her hands are armed with claws, because she is the
> insatiable goddess who is nourished by the bodies
> of men.[44]

From the preceding discussion it should be apparent
that Teódula is not a sorceress after the fashion of Consuelo, that her goals are not strictly selfish, but are rather
to fulfill the religious requirements of ritual. It is not
very important that this ritual is imposed by the worship
of an Aztec sun god instead of by the Devil. We know,
for example, that the Devil himself is seen by some biblical scholars as in part an Old Testament carry-over from
the Phoenician god, Azis, to whom the powerful effects
of the sun are ascribed, and who is thought to be the
immediate predecessor of Azazel, the desert demon in
Leviticus (16:8, 10:26).[45]

The fundamental distinction is that Teódula practices
an old religion at odds with that supposedly accepted by
society, and that like a real witch she is an agent of this
old religion, not one of its customers. Thus, although she
is an archetypal figure, she is one-sided. Whatever positive features she may have are not developed in the
novel. A minor character, in her few appearances in
Where the Air Is Clear she operates as a destructive
force, the image of the dark past with its exaltation of
sacrifice and death.

Where the Air Is Clear: *Mercedes Zamacona.* But
Fuentes has told us in his *Figaro Littéraire* interview
that there are two sorceresses in *Where the Air Is Clear*,
both based upon people he had known. Although I cannot find the Oaxacan vendor of hallucinatory mushrooms
whom he identifies as a second sorceress, there is at least

one more woman in the novel who has dark and mysterious powers. Although relatively few pages are devoted to her, in Mercedes Zamacona apparently lies the secret of Federico Robles's power (the secret that Ixca had been searching for in vain), and of Robles's fate.

Using the technique he was to use again with such success in *Artemio Cruz,* Fuentes does not reveal the secret of Robles's power until he introduces us, almost at the end of the novel, into the memories of Mercedes, Robles's first sweetheart and the mother of his child, Manuel Zamacona. It was Mercedes, pious and sensual, torn between the forces of her upbringing and the dark urging of her primitive self, who witnessed Robles's bloodletting of a horse, a ritual full of sexual implications:

> A magnetic river of power was running between the exalted flesh of the man and the animal, braided together like a broken centaur, and the triple lunar effigy of the girl; moons which pulsated, raised with all the naturalness of earth, in this moment of domination and pride . . . Mercedes closed her eyes and thought of the fist of vibrating flesh of the horse, hidden now in the boy, the man and the beast identical in the origin of power.[46]

The source of Robles's power then is as dark and ancient as Ixca's and Teódula's; and Mercedes, a woman of the earth, understands the significance of Robles's domination of the horse. In the darkness of the chapel, where the light never reached, they make love silently, and Mercedes seeks to impart still greater power to him:

> She only wanted to feed his strength, only that; to give him part of her, so that with her he could conquer horses and with her open the way with the great club between his hands, while she would tell

him that her three stars lived and had, now, a reason
for being and gave a whole world color and savor.
(p. 332, my translation)

Thus Robles nourishes his power by the sacrifice of
a horse's blood. He conquers Mercedes and her powers
are added to his own. As a revolutionary and later as a
banker, he does indeed open new roads and gather in
their fruits. But he betrays Mercedes by abandoning her
with child. Then the lovely young girl changes. The
wounds of rejection by her family, condemnation by the
priest, and solitude, harden her. By the time the child
is born she is almost a different person. And while cut-
ting the umbilical cord she sings "a song of another day,
of this future, which only in singing it later would remind
her that she had sung it then (p. 335).

She condemns the father

to darkness, that of the child's conception and birth,
to live blind, and imprisoned; condemned him to
the condemnation of his misused power, the power
she remembered in the taming of the stallion and
the flux of copulation, condemned him to a useless
trajectory, and thus in her delirium was assured that
the true fruits of his power would never be any except those of hers too, condemned him without
thought or without voice, only seeking with her
hands the missing son of the missing father, in order
to recover in the darkness his power and to use it
in the light. (p. 335)

In this curse of Mercedes we finally understand the
attraction of the blind woman, Hortensia Chacón. Only
with her in darkness can Robles find his truth, his satisfaction, his origin.[47] Again, as Mercedes has decreed,

he lives to see the vanity of his abused power. It is a power based on sacrifice, first of animal blood, then of Mercedes, then of his fellow Mexicans. Searching for him among the troops of the revolution, she knows that "his power required the conjunction of blood, of fire and of battle" (p. 338). But the day when she finally finds her son in an orphanage in Celaya, she gives up the father for dead. Fuentes does not tell us why the finding of the son should persuade her of the death of the father. He almost assumes that the reader will understand.

The Idea of Sacrifice. Implicit in Mercedes's thinking, as it was in Robles's, is the idea of sacrifice. Nothing is granted by the heavens without our paying a price. For a new life we lose an old one; the death of the father is the sacrifice required for the birth of the child. This idea is found repeatedly in Fuentes. Ludivinia in *Artemio Cruz* remembers that the child was born the day his father died. In *Where the Air is Clear*, Gervasio Pola dies the day Rodrigo Pola is born. In all three cases the young man-child replaces the older one in the heart of the woman, almost as a reincarnation. Aura, we may remember, also reminds Felipe that one must die in order to be reborn.

But in *Where the Air Is Clear*, as in *Artemio Cruz*, the sacrificial victim turns out to be the son. The death of Manuel Zamacona is on the surface a stupid, gratuitous one, as useless as the death of another, unknown man whom the destitute Robles comes upon in his wanderings through the city. But the voice and the eyes of the dead son invade the innermost recesses of the father, and for the first time he understands that the victim is his kinsman. He again identifies with the people, his people; he finds again "the truth offered in the first seed by Mercedes" (p. 338).

Far from the bone and the blood, in other lives
which at this moment of defeat and rendered flesh
were his own life, the mute lives which had fed him,
he felt the true meaning. (p. 341)

Of course there is no reason to assume that Mercedes
willed the sacrifice of her own son to effect the moral
regeneration of the father. Yet the death of the son nevertheless operates to this effect, and Mercedes, whom Robles considers a woman of "unconscious power" (p. 342),
is ultimately responsible. Thus, although she consciously willed him ill, Mercedes, through the birth and
death of her son and her curse that he find his destiny
only in darkness, is responsible for his salvation.

Mercedes as a "White" Witch. Unlike Teódula, therefore, Mercedes's role in the novel is not destructive, but
creative. Her magical powers cannot arise from a demonic, or neo-demonic source, but must be explained
differently. Mercedes can only be compared to the white
witches, the class of witch that has grown so in popularity
at the present time. These witches, according to Hill and
Williams, cannot be classified simply as sorceresses, for
although they use techniques of sorcery (as do their black
opposites), there is a quasi-religious character to their
activity. But this is neither Christian nor anti-Christian.
(They claim to be the inheritors of a pagan tradition that
antedates almost every known religion.)[48] The god of the
white witches is the Great Mother, the Earth Mother,
symbol of fertility. (Yet according to the white witches,
this is a Great Mother shorn of her negative polarity.)
However, in some cases the deity is dual, the counterpart
of the Great Mother being the Horned God, primitive
symbol of power. But the Horned God is not evil, resembling Pan more than he does Satan.[49] In such cir-

cumspect descriptions, white witches, of course, focus
only on the fertility aspect of the Great Mother.

All of Fuentes's references to the adolescent Mercedes
also associate her with the idea of fertility (as a quick
second glance at some of the already cited passages
should indicate). Even in his flashing memories of his
past, Robles's surviving impression of Mercedes is that
of a fertility symbol: "Mercedes Zamacona, warm and
dark in the midst of her siesta, convoking a wordless and
sightless meeting by her very flesh, where all seeds ger-
minated soundlessly within hands of love" (p. 342).

This ancient fertility religion was scattered throughout
the world, and some authorities suggest that it became
mingled with other religions. It can be detected in ancient Norse sagas and records of Egyptian ceremonial
magic, and mention is even made of a pre-Columbian
cult, existing in ancient Mexico. This cult is said to have
had meetings closely paralleling a sabbat, although led
by a priestess.[50] The white witches, according to their
own explanations, feel that power can be raised from
their bodies (hence the practice of performing their rites
naked, a state in which the maximum outlay of power
can be produced). Their power, practicing white witches
say, is of a psychic nature, and in the religious ecstasy
produced by their rituals they "feel themselves in contact with a supernormal power or force which in acting
together they can strengthen and direct to achieve their
desired ends."[51] Let us compare this to Mercedes's
power according to Fuentes's commentary: "And she
only wished to nourish his power, only that, to give it
part of her seed of power so that with her he would
conquer the horses. . . ."(p. 332).

Still, one might protest that the mature Mercedes is
not shown as participating in any magic rites, but rather
as living the life of a recluse. Such a life, however, is
completely compatible with the character of a white

witch, whose activities are only in part magical and
whose witchcraft is largely confined to worship.[52]

Types of Witches in Fuentes up to 1962. In Fuentes's
treatment of the witch in his earlier works, therefore, we
have both extremes in the spectrum: the witch proper
or the black witch, Teódula; and the probable white
witch, Mercedes. Ludivinia, if we ignore her rejections
of her own son, is probably also a white witch in that
she has strong psychic powers and seeks to protect Artemio Cruz, rather than to harm him. But Aura, similar
to the ghostly intruder in "Tlactocatzine," is neither
black nor white; she is merely woman and sorceress
(although her powers are greater than those of Fuentes's
witches found in a more realistic setting). Aura-Consuelo's darker side—manifest in the sacrifice of animals
for the purpose of attaining sexual powers, and anticipated in Robles's bloodletting of the horse—is almost
balanced by her need to give and receive love.

But Aura is not Fuentes's last word on the female supernatural being. In *Holy Place*, published five years
after *Aura*, the witch is again reincarnated, and this time
in her most complete and yet negative form.

III
Holy Place: The Consummate Witch

The Plot

Holy Place, Fuentes's surrealistic novel of 1967, is based on the myth of Ulysses—not the Ulysses as known in the account of Homer, but the less well-known version related by Apollodorus and retold by Robert Graves.[1] In this version, Ulysses returns to Ithaca and is again banished because of his cruel slaying of the suitors. Because of an oracle's warning to Ulysses that his own son would kill him, Telemachus is also banished. But the oracle's warning is nevertheless fulfilled when another son, this one by Circe, does in fact kill his father by mistake. A year after the father's death the guilty son, Telegonus, comes to Ithaca and marries Penelope who is still ruling there; her own son, Telemachus, marries Circe. "Thus both branches of the family became closely united."[2] In Fuentes's resumé of the myth related in the interview with Rodríguez-Monegal and published in *Mundo Nuevo*, there is a certain divergence with Apollodorus, and also new psychological details. In Fuentes's words, this is what happens:

> In fact Ulysses comes back from the war as an old man; he sits down and begins to tell stories to his

wife and his son, to wear them out with his stories, to exhaust them with so many fantastic stories that they become nervous and insane. What can Telemachus do but take up the destiny of the father, begin again the voyages of Ulysses, those voyages that will take Telemachus to the island of the sorceress Circe in the Adriatic. There he will find that he has a double, who is his brother, the son of Ulysses and Circe, Telegonus ... and in order to complete the destinies and the substitutions, Telemachus goes to bed with Circe, becomes the husband of Circe. And now it is Telegonus who continues the wanderings, the voyages that must take him to this desolate and primitive kingdom of Ithaca, where he finds the old couple, Ulysses and Penelope. Penelope sees the young Ulysses coming through the door, the one whom she saw leaving for the war. And so Penelope and Telegonus stab Ulysses, they kill him and Telegonus takes his father's place in bed. Well, this is a rough sketch of the mythical frame of reference of *Holy Place*.[3]

With such clues and all that we already know of Homer's tale, it would seem to be only a matter of fitting the details of the relationship of a Mexican movie star and her son into the original myth in order to understand the deep significance of the modern story. But there is nothing this simple in Fuentes. It is not a question of merely matching names. Any light from the earlier versions of Ulysses is deflected by the prism of twentieth-century criticism and new literary interpretations.

To take at first only a minor example, the Sirens, according to the Fuentes's narrative, did not sing:

The bound chieftain said that he had listened and resisted. He lied. It was a question of prestige, of awareness of the legend. Ulysses was his own P.R.

man. This time, and only this time, the sirens did
not sing ... Ulysses was able to pass by without
danger.[4]

Although Fuentes's debunking of the prowess of Ulysses may well be his personal interpretation, I cannot
help but compare his commentary to that by Franz Kafka
which is entitled "The Silence of the Sirens." Kafka
writes:

And when Ulysses approached them, the potent
songstresses actually did not sing, whether because
they thought that this enemy could be vanquished
only by their silence, or because the look of bliss on
the face of Ulysses, who was thinking of nothing but
his wax and his chains, made them forget their singing ... Ulysses, it is said, was so full of guile, was
such a fox, that not even the goddesses of fate could
pierce his armour ...[5]

Similarly, in the original myth Ulysses is a super-hero,
the only one to survive the hazardous journey home from
the Trojan war, a man who alone could kill a multitude
of suitors and enlist the help (and enmity) of the gods.
But in *Holy Place*, as in Joyce's *Ulysses*, he is degenerate,
bourgeois. The father of the actress's son merely writes
him a complaining letter which prompts the remark by
his ex-wife that "he was only good at selling school sup-
plies" (p. 118). Ulysses, then, becomes merely a sales-
man, despised by his wife and unloved by his son.

The Central Character: Circe

We can see that Fuentes, like so many other modern
writers, has taken great liberties with the myth of Ulysses. For him, as for Lope de Vega, the central character

is not the original hero, but Circe, the witch. And again, she is not precisely Homer's Circe. She seems rather to be a Circe inspired by Graves's short poem, "Ulysses," which contains the following stanza:

> To much-tossed Ulysses, never done
>   With woman whether gowned as wife or whore,
> Penelope and Circe seemed as one:
> She like a whore made his lewd fancies run,
>   And wifely she a hero to him bore.[6]

In this poem Penelope and Circe multiply into Scylla and Charybdis, then into the Sirens. The world of flesh and woman surrounds him, terrifies him and renders him helpless before it.

Only by reference to this kind of interpretation can I understand the Mexican movie star, Claudia, in her dual role of mother (Penelope) and witch (Circe), and the Fuentes myth of the brothers Telemachus and Telegonus who marry their father's "other" wife. If Circe is in fact Penelope, through incest Telemachus and his brother both return to the womb; both are equally deceived and enchanted by her.

If such an analysis seems highly complex, it is nevertheless the only one that fully coincides with the hints supplied by the author both in the work and in his already mentioned commentary about it.[7] The chief source of confusion and complication seems to be that the Ulysses myth is superimposed on perhaps a more basic structure. The theme of incest in *Holy Place* is far stronger than that of adventure and quest, characteristic of the Odyssey (although, of course, there is in Fuentes's novel the element of quest on the part of "Mito," the son, for some kind of personal identity). Still, we seem to be dealing far more with *Oedipus Rex* than with Ulysses, but an *Oedipus* doubled in two of its basic characters and dominated by the female heroine. Only by a detailed study of this overwhelming character, Claudia Nervo, is it possible to understand the deeper layers of meaning in *Holy Place.*

The Witch as Hermaphrodite

So far I have suggested that Claudia is more than one person, that like Consuelo of *Aura* she can project herself into other forms; that she is in fact all women, or the archetype of woman as mother, mistress, wife. What remains to be seen is that Claudia not only has doubles but is herself a double, part female and part male. Again I must refer to Jung, who pointed out that "man in his myths always manifested the idea of the coexistence of male and female in the same body. Such pschological intuitions were usually projected in the form of the divine *Syzygia,* the divine pair, or the idea of the hermaphroditic nature of the creator."[8]

In literary terms, Northrop Frye also discusses hermaphroditism (plus incest and homosexuality—all elements present in *Holy Place*) as a leading component in the demonic, erotic relation which is fiercely destructive and "is symbolized by a harlot, witch, siren or other tantalizing female."[9]

That Claudia is in fact hermaphroditic is strongly hinted by Severo Sarduy, the only critic I have found who has penetrated deeply beneath the surface of *Holy Place.* In his article entitled "Un Fetiche de Cachemira," he observes:

There is no reference to Claudia's hands . . . to her body in its opacity, her material presence; only her manner of speaking is recorded . . . her rough gestures of straight lines, decisive, virile; a voice which

someone in the group of fanatics compares to that
of a sergeant; her rapid, firm way of walking . . . her
significance is that of a motionless face in its iconic
authority.[10]

One of the characters in the novel even remarks,
"Don't you find that there is something very masculine
about her?" (p. 98).

According to Sarduy, part of Claudia's fascination is
due to terror, the terror of the horror films and the technique of close-up where we feel ourselves swallowed
up in the human image: "The face of Claudia owes its
magnetism to terror, to terror it owes the perfection that
her son wishes to attract, to incorporate inside himself,
to annul, as if to fill out his own empty visage."[11] "Mito,"
the son, confirms the words of Sarduy: "Known for her
beauty, the Medusa demands to be recognized for her
horror" (p. 120).

But besides the terror, and perhaps participating in it,
is the fascination of Claudia as an archetype: "Not a
woman, but a concept, a carnal essence, something both
clear and neutral. Neutral not because it is asexual . . .
but because in it the sexes meet and do battle."[12] Again,
it is "Mito" who says of her, "In her opposites fuse; you
are I; all of us are another" (p. 142).

Like the earlier witches in Fuentes's work, therefore,
Claudia is anima, a fusion of opposites, the archetype of
life itself. Compared to her vitality, the bevy of starlets
who surround her are two-dimensional. Only Bela, the
Italian beauty (who must be Penelope if the modern
story is to duplicate in any degree the version of Apollodorus), manages momentarily to incarnate Claudia and
as such both repels and attracts "Mito." "Mito" comes
as close as he can to absorption of the maternal figure
by a sexual relationship with her shadow, Bela—a relationship that he then flaunts in Claudia's face. But his

purpose is frustrated, as is his attempt through fetishism to physically incorporate Claudia within himself—to become Claudia in order to become himself. His amateurish magic (and this is what one might consider fetishism within the novel's context) provokes the anger of the witch, and "Mito" becomes completely insane. The viewpoint of the narrator, "Mito," in the last few chapters is that of a dog. Yet given the surrealistic technique of the novel, it is far from clear whether "Mito" now merely believes himself to be a dog, punished in the very way he once punished his own pets, or if his body has suffered a Kafka-esque mutation. In *Holy Place*, either or any hypothesis is possible. Since "Mito" is our only source of information, fact and fantasy are never untangled. At any rate, the narrator remains in the sacred zone of his apartment, tended only by his profane servant girl and her brutish lover. But he is forever banished from the presence of Claudia, the true "sacred zone" of which the apartment was only an imitation.

The Multiple Meanings behind the Title *Holy Place*

A deeper meaning of the holy place is indicated by Sarduy:

> The sifted light of the holy place, which mother-of-pearl and thick lamp shades filter, is meant to evoke that of the mother's home and metaphorically that of the initial cloister . . . thus it must be the interior of the maternal womb . . .[13]

The holy place, therefore, is more than a physical refuge from the outside world. "Mito" in describing it talks of a circle into which "the epidemic cannot enter. . . . The holy place isolates me and continues me; the profane remains outside" (p. 30). Instinctively he senses the sacred nature of the circle which, according to Jung, is the archetypal image of the deity, an image that asserts itself to the unconscious mind.[14] On the deepest possible level the holy place can refer to God, whose circular symbol (the microcosm, a point, and the macrocosm, the universe) is echoed in the maternal womb. So viewed, the myth of *Holy Place* is universal in the most literal sense. Yet there is also a parochial significance to the title, and this, for the purpose of the study of Claudia as hermaphrodite, is by far the most interesting.

Since the holy place is Claudia's womb, and Claudia is herself a symbol of Mexico ("before, Mexico was Pancho Villa, now it's me" [p. 31]), her womb can also be considered Mexico itself, sacred motherland and birthplace of "Mito." The myth of Claudia and her son is, at least in part, also a Mexican myth, and when it is so viewed the hermaphroditic nature of the sex goddess becomes even more obvious.

Mexican Mythology and its Analogy to the Ulysses of Apollodorus (the Interpretation of Octavio Paz)

A brief reference to the insights of Octavio Paz concerning Mexican history and mythology, insights with which Fuentes is highly familiar, will do much to explain the nature of Claudia. Among the many myths that enter into the Mexican psyche is the myth of the dispossessed, the Mexicans or Aztecs, whose conquest by the Spaniards was greatly facilitated by their belief that they had already been abandoned by their own gods.[15] Montezuma surrendered, suggests Paz, because he was strangely fascinated by the Spaniards and felt before them a kind of dizziness which could unexaggeratedly be called awe.[16] In like manner, I would suggest that Claudia abandons "Mito" in the interest of her career and that, like Montezuma, "Mito" feels a strange fascination for the rival and double, Giancarlo (Telégono), who is to replace him in the favor of the goddess.

To continue the analogy with Mexican history, Cuauhtémoc ("eagle who falls") assumes power after the death of Montezuma only to fall again quickly, as becomes a mythical hero. Paz observes: "Even his relationship with a woman fits the archetype of the young hero, at one and the same time the lover and son of the goddess."[17] "Mito" 's double, Giancarlo, then, in his incestuous relationship with the goddess and his rapid fall (as predicted by "Mito" at the conclusion of the novel) also suggests the role of Cuauhtémoc. Between them the twin brothers ("Brothers born of the same mother ... Guglielmo:Apollo ... and his antagonist twin, Dionysus ..." [p. 86]) form a composite picture of the last two Aztec emperors. Even the device of the double male hero has roots in Mexican mythology. One of the leading gods of the ancient Mexican pantheon, Quetzalcoatl (god of wind, of life, of the morning, and of the planet Venus) is also the god of twins and of monsters. His very name means precious twin, "gemelo precioso"—a name meant to indicate that the morning and evening star are one and the same.[18]

"Mito" and Giancarlo, therefore, have their prototypes in Mexican history and mythology. In various degrees they are Montezuma, Cuauhtémoc, Quetzalcoatl and the twin stars of morning and evening. But how are we to identify the heroine, the movie star Claudia, in strictly Mexican terms? Is she any of the particular goddesses of the old Aztec pantheon, any of the ones who betrayed the Mexicans and brought about their defeat?

Although as mother Claudia abandons "Mito," as goddess she cannot be assimilated to any of the male warrior gods responsible for the Aztecs's defeat. "With the defeat of these Gods," says Paz, "one cosmic cycle closes and a new divine reign begins, producing among the faithful a kind of return to the ancient female divinities."[19] Is Claudia, then, part of the cult of return to the female womb manifest in the rapid popularity that the Virgin achieved after the conquest? If we bear in mind the importance of Claudia's womb, she may perhaps be assimilated to the role of the Virgin of Guadalupe with whom she is compared by Fuentes. For "Mito," for Giancarlo, she is refuge, shelter, protection from the outside, mortal world. And yet she is much more than this. She is horror and terror, life-destroying and life-giving, the fusion of opposites of which "Mito"-dog speaks. Paz says of the archetypal mother as seen by the Mexican Indian that "like all mothers, she is affection, repose, return to the beginning, and by the same token, mouth that devours, woman who mutilates and punishes; terrible mother."[20]

This is certainly not the Virgin as explained in the Catholic doctrine. The origins of Claudia as goddess must be found much further back in Mexican history than the Christian period. She is, as we have seen, womb, mother earth, Mexico in symbol and in fact. In *La Religión de los Aztecas*, Alfonso Caso says that for Mexicans the earth is a kind of monster usually represented in the form of a goddess, variously known as Coatlicue, Cihuacoatl, or Tlazotleotl. Her names mean, "she of the skirt of serpents, woman serpent, or Goddess of uncleanliness."[21]

Coatlicue (as mentioned in the discussion of Teódula Moctezuma) is the insatiable goddess who feeds on men's bodies, and for this reason she is called the eater of filth, "la comedora de inmundicias". Her entire figure, says Caso, is an admirable synthesis of ideas of love and destruction.[22]

As Cihuacoatl, she is patron of women who die in childbirth and who return to the earth on certain days to frighten wayfarers and children. In popular Mexican mythology, Cihuacoatl has been transformed into "la llorona" who carries a crib or the body of a child, and who shrieks bitterly in the night. But as eater of filth she has a positive side in that she eats men's sins, leaving them clean (thus the affinity of the Mexican soul for confessions).[23] Claudia, like Coatlicue, therefore, is clearly a manifestation of the Earth Mother with all her positive and negative features, life-giving and life-destroying qualities. She is a complete goddess, unlike the other great Mexican female symbols, the Virgin of Guadalupe and "La Chingada," the violated one, who is represented in the modern Mexican mentality by la Malinche, the Indian guide of Cortés. The Virgin and "La Chingada," according to Paz, are the official and unofficial female archetypes in modern Mexico, but they cater only to one side of the Mexican's needs and character.[24] They protect and comfort, but they are incomplete mothers in that they have no control over evil or violence as man experiences them in his everyday life. Yet the old fertility goddesses, of whom Coatlicue is one, who were associated with the agrarian society have lost their relevance. Given such circumstances, the role of Claudia, the "sex goddess," takes on tremendous importance. Her sexuality is understood not in the sense of reproduction, although, like the Virgin, she has also produced a child, but in the purely lascivious sense. Her model in reality, as George McMurray points out, is the actress María Félix, who, like Claudia, is rumored to maintain a strange relationship with her son.[25] Fuentes mythifies this relationship, exaggerates it in the fashion that pop art exaggerates all the coarseness and false values of modern society. In a way he also dignifies it by drawing parallels with Greek mythology. Satirizing it, he also elevates it to symbol, gives it universal meaning. But whereas in its analyses of the Oedipus myth (its latent cannibalism in which the son longs not only to merge with, but to consume, the mother figure, to become her and in fact replace her), *Holy Place* can be seen as universal in theme, in its representation of Claudia as hermaphrodite, the novel has an especially Mexican aspect. The image of the serpent, we may remember, is suggestive not only of the Gorgon with whom Claudia is compared by Fuentes, but particularly of Coatlicue, creator and destroyer, serpent woman, symbol of the earth.

Claudia as "La Chingadora"

In Claudia we find the antithesis of "La Chingada," the passive, defenseless violated female. Claudia might instead be called "La Chingadora" or "La Chingona," for in her relationships with men she is the aggressor, the violator, "la devoradora de hombres." She is not only Coatlicue, but something more.

A pantheon of male gods, many destructive, all virile, coexisted with Coatlicue. The work of destruction, the powers of life and death, were rationed in the old Aztec world, divided among many deities.

But the male gods, as Paz points out, betrayed the Mexicans, leaving them finally only the consolation of the passive virgin and the violated mother, the consolation of a defeated and orphaned race. The power for effecting violence and destruction was inherited by the Spaniards, who encouraged the Indians to worship the passive female figure. But the Mexicans are a violent, emotional people. With revolution, with the stirring sense of nationhood and the new chauvinism, it is only natural that the Mexican should look for new heroes, new idols. And since the male ones bear the onus of betrayal and defeat, why not a female one who combines the attributes of both sexes, a complete god of love and hatred, birth and death, destruction and creation? These have been the requirements for a deity from earliest times. Mircea Eliade traces the ancient history of the androgynous or hermaphroditic deity, suggests its roots in prehistory, and shows how it corresponds to a human need for completeness. The isolated individual feels incomplete in limited maleness or femaleness, and visualizing his gods as perfect, he sees them as combining all opposites.[26]

Claudia as a modern screen idol, a modern goddess, therefore, combines attributes which man has always assigned to the beings he adored. On the mythical level she may be considered a highly typical goddess with prototypes in Greek, Mexican, and other mythologies. But she is not only a goddess. In several scenes Fuentes also treats her as a woman.

On the level of realism, Claudia has her prototype in earlier creations of Fuentes. As hermaphrodite, her male characteristics often parallel those of Artemio Cruz. Like him, she is the ruthless betrayer who has risen to the heights by coldly using her friends and acquaintances. Like him, she is vital and magnetic, and all those around her are pale by comparison. Like Cruz, Claudia is described as of mestizo origin, coming from the provinces, "from a land of cattlemen and revolutionaries, of horsemen" (p. 22). She is admired by foreigners, but despises them (especially the Americans). As a financial magnate, like Cruz and like Federico Robles, she has important interests in Mexico and in the United States: "We'll get Texas back yet," she jests with her secretary (p. 40).

On the level of realism, *Holy Place* contains the same

biting criticism of Mexican society that *Where the Air Is Clear* and *Artemio Cruz* had highlighted before. We see in Claudia an archetype, a celluloid character, yet having more substance than the world of hangers-on who surround her. She has at least the virtue of being genuinely herself. Like the earth, she corrupts and feeds on corruption, but the people around her are no better than shadows. And unlike Artemio Cruz or Federico Robles, Claudia has never sold out a revolution. She is the old, not the new. She is the old order of cacique, oppressor, violator, the old order which has always dwelt beneath the surface of Mexican life. In this she partially resembles Consuelo, the spiritual mother of Aura. But if we are to employ the distinction between witch and sorceress suggested in the discussion of the earlier work, Claudia is definitely a witch. Her goal is largely power for its own sake. From her admirers she desires not love, but adulation. She is not, of course, a worshipper of the Devil, but is herself a kind of she-devil to whom her court of apprentice witches must pay homage.

Claudia as Witch

The theme of Claudia as witch is so obvious that it hardly requires commentary. There is evidence on nearly every page to remind us that Claudia is Circe, or Medea, or a Mexican witch painted by Leonora Carrington (p. 15). Her secretary Ruth is variously described as both "incubus" and "familiar," terms associated with witches. Ruth's description as an incubus or male demon sent by Satan to lead women into sexual sin (added to her masculine appearance, "her eternal tailored suit," "her short hair" [p. 24]) strongly suggests a lesbian relationship with Claudia. As a "familiar" or personal demon employed by witches to focus and strengthen their power, she is seen finally by "Mito" with her true face, that of a monkey (p. 143). And Ruth is not the only "familiar" in Claudia's household. A far more potent "familiar" is the rat that Claudia keeps imprisoned in a glass tube, the rat whose contemplation by "Mito" results in his metamorphosis into a dog. In an earlier scene with the same caged rat, we see through "Mito's" eyes how Claudia and the rat hypnotize each other; there are incantations before the animal. She seems to be training the rat for its magical role. In this scene all the modern window dressing is removed from Claudia, and she is revealed as the true witch she is, powerful enough to effect total change in others and through her "familiar" to be changed herself. She says to the rat, "I am tired of seeing myself, . . . But I'm not tired of being seen. When I get tired, you will change. Look how I look, look how I look at myself. . . ." (p. 97).

It is this power of Claudia's of entering into others, of taking them over either in body or soul, that is sensed by Bela. And despite Claudia's enormous attraction for her, she begins to fear their relationship. She writes to Guillermo ("Mito"):

> there is something worse than you in this house, I prefer you because I know what you are, not something that also threatens me in this house with your mother . . . you must save me, accepting what I can give you, before I begin to believe that you and your mother have planned all this together . . ." (p. 90, 91)

To characterize Claudia's relationship with her court (or harem, as she calls it) as merely lesbian, therefore, is to fail to see its deeper implication. Claudia possesses

others spiritually; she can *become* them, and it is this
loss of personality, this psychic intrusion, that Bela
seems to fear rather than any physical impropriety.

The Role of Bela

Bela's fear may, of course, be premonition or intuition.
But in view of other hints given us by the author, it may
also be reawakened memory.

As "Mito" warned in the first days of his courtship
with Bela, "If you recognize me, you'll stop existing"
(p. 25). By Bela's sly remark to "Mito" that one of her
friends is Giancarlo ("Mito" 's twin), Fuentes suggests
that Bela has in fact long been associated with Claudia,
has been used body and soul by Claudia in the past.
Suddenly "Mito" understands the identity of Bela:

> She has no need, in the end, to show her face. I
> guessed it because I feared it. . . . She shows it as
> she gets out of the car, slams the door violently and
> repeats:
>   "Giancarlo Adelphi."
> She reveals to me her immodesty, her loose, black
> hair, obviously dyed, perhaps a wig, her arched, ar-
> tificial eyebrows, shaped just so, in imitation . . . she
> smiles at me so that I can recognize myself in her
> again, as I recognized myself in the woman in the
> perfumed fox boa who kidnapped me from my
> grandmother's house. Disguised as Claudia and
> then disguised as myself and with that name on her
> lips, denying all my uniqueness, invading my prop-
> erty, mocking my identity. . . . (p. 28)

Even in the love scene between Bela and "Mito," he
tries to distinguish between the "real" Bela, "la verdad-

era" who walks beside him, and the other one whom he
fears. He asks himself: "Wasn't her imitation only prophetic salvation of something she was supposed to copy
in order to avoid living?" (p. 52). And again "Mito" reminds himself, "I have to repeat to myself that I met her
before, then, not now as she is" (p. 52).

Bela, therefore, has at least a double role in *Holy Place*.
On the one hand, she is the "real" Bela, a spontaneous,
passionate, freethinking Italian starlet—on the other, a
creature of Claudia with only vague premonitions of
herself in the other role. And it is as the real Bela that
she both fears, and is attracted to, Claudia. As the "other
one" she *is* Claudia, body and soul. We see that Bela in
her weakness is attracted by Claudia's strength (just as
Ruth and "Mito" are), but it is this same strength that
she fears intuitively as destructive of her personality.
Yet Bela is more fortunate than "Mito." Essentially het-
erosexual, seeking fulfillment in someone outside herself, she desires to belong to "Mito." But "Mito," unfortunately, is only a pale reflection of Claudia. Incomplete
without her, he needs only Claudia, does not feel fully
alive without her.

Other Hermaphrodites

Mito. In fact, "Mito" is an unsuccessful hermaphrodite
and thus appears arrested at a narcissistic form of development. This is recognized by Bela when she writes
to "Mito":

> You no longer see what the rest of us are, the men
> and women who don't join your horrible, solitary
> game .... I don't know how to look at myself in
> mirrors, nobody lives in mirrors ... (p. 90)

Even "Mito" recognizes his apparently narcissistic tendencies in which he tries to substitute his own body for Claudia's presence. Just as Bela charges, "Mito" is a "monster" who needs no contact with reality himself and seeks to prevent her contact with it by magic means:

> You will continue threatening me as long as I live and as long as you compel me to think that I can find you again, with another face, disguised, ready to deprive me of my beautiful contact with everything that really exists. . . . (p. 90)

We have already seen "Mito's" flirtation with magic in his fetishistic practices with Claudia's clothes. "Mito's" problem seems to be that he is a frustrated, unsuccessful witch or wizard, and though he spies on Claudia to learn her magic tricks, he has not learned enough. Like Claudia, for example, he sacrifices animals in magic rites (Claudia's rug is covered with the dismembered bodies of animals [p. 97]), but his tossing of his pet dogs into the path of onrushing cars only provokes his mother's disdain. His whole relationship with his animals, in fact, is almost a parody of Claudia's relationship with her starlet hangers-on. Like her, he refers to them as his *corte* ("court"), and he is completely arbitrary as to which shall be sacrificed, which rewarded. As gifts from Claudia, the dogs are seen by him as transitory incarnations in dog form of "ancient, forgotten, irreproducible" faces (p. 35; the English version omits this phrase). Perhaps they are intended to remind us of Circe's swine, with "Mito" in the unflattering role of swineherd.

Giancarlo. But if "Mito" is an unsuccessful witch and hermaphrodite, the twin (Giancarlo) is not very different. He too has his *holy place* in an inner chamber of an old Italian palazzo, where his movements and attire remind

"Mito" of "the God Pan in Versailles."[27] Spying on Giancarlo as he has on Claudia, "Mito" observes him performing magic rites and sexual aberrations with life-sized dolls (all pregnant), which he himself has created. Also a hermaphrodite in desire, if not in fact, Giancarlo is seen in the role of a woman about to give birth:

> You moved away from the doll, rolled over, ended face up, with your legs opened, arched, resting on your elbows. And the childbirth . . . was of the being who comes back each time we forget him, of the being who has died before and will always die from time to time in order not to resemble a monster: you sweat, twist slowly, beneath the gaze of the fat angels and the vampires, of the art that you inherited and the art that you created. . . . (p. 82).

Yet unlike a somewhat similar scene in *Change of Skin* in which a witch gives birth to a stuffed doll, in the case of Giancarlo it is a false labor. As witch, as hermaphrodite, he too is frustrated. The dolls he creates he must fabricate by hand. He cannot produce them biologically, in spite of his inherited arts. Although he assumes the role of woman in order to reproduce, in order to survive ("I want to survive," he explains, "I am searching for the only way that I know how" [p. 82]), his "womb" is barren. He cannot be self-sufficient.

As his twin, Giancarlo reflects the dilemma of "Mito" who desires to contain Claudia within himself in order to overcome her. "Mito" tries to fall in love with the part of himself that is woman. His self-lovemaking is the counterpart of Giancarlo's self-induced "pregnancy":

> I caress myself slowly and see myself freed of other's desires; alone in my enchanted grotto, soon to turn into desire itself: *putto*, immaculate angel who will

take neither husband nor wife, aloof cherub. I open
my legs in a great Y of egoistic liberation: childish
and sick. . . . (p. 75)

Thus, although the relationship of each twin with himself could be termed "narcissistic" and the relationship
between them contains elements of narcissism (in that
each sees himself reflected in the other) as well as of
homosexuality, it would be incorrect to summarize the
important relationships in *Holy Place* in largely Freudian terms. Even the mother-son relationship, which I
have already termed an Oedipus relationship, should not
receive a Freudian interpretation.[28]

The Metaphysical Goal

Although there is a strong sexual element present in
Holy Place, its role is largely a means to something else
rather than an end in itself. In all the characters from
Claudia to Giancarlo, rather than lasciviousness, there
is an anguish to survive, to find some kind of immortality.
Although symbols are inverted, and Giancarlo, for example, has a portrait of a vampire above his bedstead
instead of a virgin, there is nevertheless a search for
meaning in life, a search which is essentially religious
in nature. This search is reflected in the very title of the
book. For these reasons it should not seem strange if the
parallels that we find in *Holy Place* come not only from
Mexican and Greek mythology, and from modern literary
interpretations of classical myths, but also from the Bible. To summarize, therefore: The original myth behind
Holy Place is Apollodorus's version of *Ulysses*. Struc-
tured somewhat precariously upon this is the weight of
twentieth-century literary interpretations, chiefly those
of Graves and Joyce's *Ulysses*. As Joyce split Ulysses in

two, his intellectual and his sensual halves,[29] Fuentes
splits the son of Ulysses in two, "Mito" and Giancarlo,
and the wife or mistress, Circe, into two principal emanations. Although the leading exponent of Circe is
Claudia, she can also be incarnated in Bela (Penelope).
By this I do not mean to imply that Fuentes is necessarily
imitating either Joyce or Graves. The technique of the
double, or the shadow, as Jung sometimes calls it, seems
to be part of the patrimony we all share, although most
Jungians would assign it to the personal, rather than the
collective, unconscious. Certainly, it is also a favorite
archetype of Borges, Cortázar, García-Marquez, etc.
Fuentes utilizes it with at least as much frequency as
the anima. From "Tlactocatzine, del Jardín de Flandes"
through to his latest novels, Fuentes depicts as many
male shadow figures as animas, and there is no more
need to look for "sources" in the one case than in the
other.

As Jung points out in his own study of Ulysses:

> The artist is the spokesman for the psychic secrets
> of his period, an involuntary one, as any authentic
> prophet, at times unconscious as a sleepwalker. He
> has the illusion that he speaks for himself, but the
> one who speaks through his lips is the spirit of his
> times . . . the unconscious has been known to play
> jokes on the author in spite of his numerous
> precautions.[30]

Perhaps one of the jokes that the unconscious plays on
Fuentes is in supplying him with a half forgotten
"source" from the book of Genesis.

It is the influence of woman that leads "Mito" to sin.
As Claudia, she denies his personality, tempts and frustrates him. As Bela, she seduces him and tricks him into
the sin of incest. And as mother again, she punishes him

for it by changing him into an animal. As Hermione says, "The bitch mother . . . gave birth to the serpent and with the serpent gave herself over to enjoyment of sex, and the serpent believed himself to be the true creator but she showed him. . . . " (p. 131). And Kirsten, another member of what we may compare to a Greek chorus, adds: "She crushed his skull with a kick, she kicked out his teeth and exiled him to the black caverns of the black world" (p. 132). "Mito," then, becomes the serpent in his own modern garden of Eden, his sacred zone, but his fate is that of victim as well as tempter. As a symbol of demonic imagery, he would represent the *pharmakos,* or sacrificial victim, who, according to Northrop Frye, must be killed to strengthen the others.[31] Although he is not actually killed in the story, he is expelled from the sacred presence, and this amounts to the same thing. "Mito," like Adam,[32] has been guilty of disobedience (to Claudia, who plays the roles of both God and Eve) and presumption. He has tried to taste the fruits of knowledge—the occult secrets guarded by Claudia—and so he must be expelled. The message is the same as in Genesis (Man is weak and easily beguiled. Woman is the source of temptation—and evil), but goes beyond Genesis. Even evil on this earth is innocent. As "Mito" laments at the story's end: "What's terrible is to know the witch is innocent and for that she is guilty . . . that we can't live without her and we can't live with her" (p. 141). The stake is never justified. Claudia, like most of Fuentes's other witches, is a necessary, innocent evil.

IV
Change of Skin

In *Holy Place*, Fuentes writes on the level of myth from beginning to end. There is no gradual immersion of the real world into the mythical one, as we found, for example, in *Aura*. Although Fuentes has said that in *Holy Place* he elaborates a myth, "based on elements of reality,"[1] all the characters of the novel are components of myth, and have magical powers. Having created such a consummate witch as Claudia Nervo in such a fully developed mythical atmosphere, one might suppose that Fuentes had said his last word on the subject and would turn again to a more realistic approach to social problems (although not necessarily to the Galdós-like style he uses in *The Good Conscience*). Yet the next novel published, *Cambio de piel* (*Change of Skin*), is not a "realistic" novel.

Originally titled *El sueño* (*The Dream*), *Change of Skin*, according to the critic Joseph Sommers, was begun in 1963 and scheduled for publication in 1966.[2] Actually published in August 1967 (five months later than *Holy Place*) after extensive revisions, it is a work that could be considered either antecedent to, or a development of, the shorter novel *Holy Place*, which Fuentes regarded as an experiment.[3]

The Theme of Woman as Witch

Ophelia, the Mother. With respect to the theme of woman as witch, the first part of *Change of Skin* (which in length is some three-fourths of the novel) reminds one of the handling of the same theme in many of Fuentes's works prior to *Holy Place.* Ophelia, the mother of the protagonist, Javier, is both *young* and *old* ("with her face of a girl grown old. . . ."[4]), and has the same incestuous feelings for her son that we saw, for example, between Rosenda Pola and her son Rodrigo in *Where the Air Is Clear.*

Elizabeth, Dragona-Ligeia. Just as other women in his works have invented parts of their past (Regina in *The Death of Artemio Cruz* invents the episode of her meeting Artemio at the seaside in order to glamorize shabby reality), Elizabeth, the heroine, seems to have invented her entire past as she explains it, in order to awaken Javier's imagination (p. 374).[5] Although we learn more about Elizabeth than about any other character, since she is the focal point of the story, we cannot ever be sure who she really is. For this she blames her husband, Javier:

> Do you think I'm still Elizabeth Jonas, the girl you met in New York? Don't you see that I've become you yourself? What you wanted me to become. That I speak and think now not as myself but as you? That I have no personality of my own? (p. 325)

She is perhaps the ghost of woman that Octavio Paz describes in his *Labyrinth of Solitude:*

> Between ourselves and Woman there is interposed a Ghost, that of her image, that of the image that we

create of her and with which she clothes herself.
. . . And to woman the same thing happens.
. . . she does not feel or conceive of herself except
as an object, an "other." She is never mistress of
herself.[6]

But at least she is aware of her subservient condition
and protests. In the words of "la Pálida," the hippie
actress who portrays Elizabeth in the final section of the
book, "Can no one love me for myself? Must I always
be the repetition of a nightmare or the anticipation of a
dream for a man to love me?" (p. 412). Yet Elizabeth is
not defenseless. She hints of dark and hidden powers:

Don't tempt me, Javier. Don't make me do you real
harm. . . . Don't tell me that everything good I owe
to you, because I am going to answer you with something bad. (p. 333, English; p. 331 Spanish versions)

On the surface this appears only an idle threat in a
matrimonial quarrel, yet in the mind of Javier, at least,
there is strong suspicion of his wife's occult powers.
Denying his own words of love for her, he charges, "I
repeated aloud what you used to say to me in secret, at
night, tigress, witch . . . Ligeia. . . . (p. 328, Spanish version; the English version on page 331 omits this line).
He accuses her of robbing him of his virility, a frequent
charge against witches: "You have turned me into a sterile ruin" (p. 328). He suspects her of practicing secret
rites:

Do you think I'm blind? That I didn't see you hiding
at the foot of the pyramid trying to wrap the stone
serpent around you? (p. 326)[7]
Do you think I didn't see Franz deceiving us so that

you could carry out your hellish rite? (p. 323, Spanish version only)

The very names he calls her suggest magic and evil:
"Dragona," "Ligeia." Commenting on the symbol of
dragon in demonic imagery, Northrop Frye says:

> The dragon is especially appropriate because it is
> not only monstrous and sinister but fabulous, and
> so represents the paradoxical nature of evil as a
> moral fact and an eternal negation.[8]

Her mythical, half-evil nature is further confirmed in her
second nickname, "Ligeia." This was the name of one
of the Sirens, the creatures who were half-bird, half-
woman, and who tried to lure Ulysses to his doom. Ligeia
is also the name of Edgar Allan Poe's supernatural heroine in the story that is so entitled. Poe's Ligeia, too, is
of mysterious origin (even for her husband), is exceed-
ingly wise and learned, and is able to reincarnate herself
in the body of his young wife. In all this the Ligeia of
Fuentes provides a close parallel.

Yet we need not look beyond Fuentes's own works to
find the inspiration for Elizabeth. She is the natural descendent of Tlactocatzine, of Aura-Consuelo. She is, in
short, a new incarnation of the anima. There is a certain
timelessness about her, although it is subtler than in our
earlier examples. She is merely proud of her youthful
figure, and almost brags to her husband that she looks
exactly as she did twenty years before. But basically she
is insecure in this youthfulness, because it is not enough
for Javier.

She tries to pretend she is another woman in order to
excite his former passion:

> You desire that this night he love you as if you were
> another; it doesn't matter that he call you by another
> name in bed. . . . The only thing that matters is this
> passion that you find together after he has forgotten
> you and found another (p. 244)

The problem, therefore, is not only to be young, but also
to be *new*. And even this Elizabeth can accomplish. Like
Consuelo, she reincarnates her youth. In the words of
the narrator:

> So one day youth enters the apartment. Your own
> youth . . .
> For several hours, several days, you succeed in
> maintaining that reincarnated image from your past.
> And what do you do with it? You use it to make love.
> You become young again and now you can make
> love truly, through the phantom that is you with all
> the experience added, the nostalgia, the retrospec-
> tive desire that you could not feel when you were
> truly young. . . .(p. 172)

In Elizabeth we have a character who is by her own
confession a ghost, who dilutes her reality still further
by conjuring up a new ghost in order to win fully the
love of a man who will reveal to her what she feared,
that it was only *his* ghost whom she loved (p. 173).

If there was one ghost looking over Fuentes's shoulder
in *Aura*, in *Change of Skin* there are at least three. It is
not surprising that the novel was first called *The Dream*.
But perhaps even more appropriate is the final title,
Change of Skin, evocative of the serpent of Mexico's
mythical past, the creature who repeatedly changes skins
but remains essentially the same.

The Plot

The dream-like quality, the uncertainty of the earlier novels is magnified to the point that it is almost impossible to give a résumé of "plot" since this is largely left up to the reader. The author merely sets the stage on the road to and in the Mexican town of Cholula, and through the intervention of a usually invisible narrator reports the apocryphal memories of the heroine, Elizabeth (memories which we should finally realize are merely episodes of movies she has seen). But as to the actual conclusion of the relationship between husband and wife, several possible endings are suggested, and presumably the reader will pick the one corresponding best to his understanding of the story, as well as his intuition as to how many "real"[9] characters are represented in the novel.

The Characters: Real and Unreal

It is my understanding that there are three such relatively "real" characters, Elizabeth, Javier, and Franz. "White Rabbit," who becomes Elizabeth in the last section of the novel is, I believe, only intended to represent a mental projection of the narrator, an interpretation to be dealt with in the section on "the Monks." Franz, the ex-Nazi, although described by Fuentes as the other face of Javier,[10] in my opinion turns out to be a genuine character (at least insofar as any character in this novel may be so designated), and may, in fact, be the only one with memories of a factual past (rather than one superimposed by the movies).

With respect to character identification, the main problems are Elizabeth's young rival, Isabel, and the narrator himself. The problem of the narrator is so complicated

that it is best dealt with at the conclusion of this discussion. For the moment I shall only point out that the
narrator is in fact both narrator and character, his
identity being further confused by Fuentes himself, who
says that the narrator could be any one of the characters.[11]

As for Isabel, the main problem is whether she is the
product of Elizabeth's witchery or the Narrator's. Fuentes
says she is "a repetition of Elizabeth at another time,
with another rhythm,"[12] but he does not tell us *whose*
creation she is.

At first we only suspect that Isabel knows she is enchanted—although she may express this knowledge as
a joke: "Let's pretend we're enchanted! . . . Come touch
me, Javier! Break the spell!" (pp. 32, 33). But Javier,
undoubtedly referring to Elizabeth and himself answers:

> "First remember that she has a face covered by the
> mask of a skeleton and that he is waiting for you
> surrounded by owls and spiders and that at his side
> is his wife with a living face underneath the mask
> of death." (p. 33, English, p. 40, Spanish)

If Elizabeth is the creator of Isabel, she is a sorcerer's
apprentice who has begun something she cannot control.
She warns Javier about her young rival:

> "Franz is merely looking for something he has lost
> a long time ago. I know. I am looking for the love
> you stopped giving me. Only Isabel is the danger.
> Only she is looking toward the future, not back-
> ward . . . ."(p. 327)

Elizabeth as the creator of Isabel hardly makes sense
psychologically, unless we concede that Elizabeth is
either a very inexpert witch (far less adept than Consuelo, who at least controlled her younger self), or else

that what Elizabeth wants is precisely to suffer the rivalry of Isabel in order to test Javier, or that she has a masochistic desire to drink the last bitter drops in her relationship with her husband.

But more evidence seems to suggest that Isabel is not the creation of Elizabeth, but of the Narrator who controls her far better than he does his other characters. Using her as a tool, he sets the scene for the decisive episode in the pyramid where the execution of Franz (her lover and also Elizabeth's) is to take place; he counts on her to make Franz reveal the history of unknown Nazi criminals, now dead. She is responsible for introducing the monks, the hippie order composed of characters even further removed from reality than herself. Like them, she is a catalyst; she effects changes in the lives of others without becoming personally involved. She is, in fact, so adept at simulating reality that she becomes for Javier more real than Elizabeth. And Elizabeth feels this and suffers; in one of their quarrels, reproaching Javier:

> Now you can go to a real woman. With a name, Isabel. Before you were searching for a ghost. . . . I. Your ghost. I loved you. But you have never loved women. You have loved The Woman. With capitals. A ghost. Only that way you felt free. (p. 335, Spanish version)

Isabel even imagines at times that she is real and that her destiny lies with Javier. But Javier knows at last that she is Elizabeth all over again: "Isabel is Ligeia, Isabel will be Ligeia . . . . Will bring me back to the hell of Ligeia" (p. 381).

Yet he requires this inferno of Ligeia: "She doesn't understand that Ligeia, his poison, is also his life, his habit, that without that habit his world would collapse" (p. 380).

The Themes

Javier, then, like Felipe Montero in *Aura,* accepts his subjection to woman as witch, as love goddess, "so that man and woman can tie themselves together, kill each other, rob each other of their solitary identity" (p. 329). The themes of *Aura* are orchestrated here with an additional couple and more verbal pyrotechnics, but they are basically the same. Instead of an old mansion where limited sacrifice is performed, we have an old pyramid where sacrifice has been performed on a grandiose scale. But both house and pyramid are symbols of Mexico's past, consciously often forgotten, but subconsciously very much alive and not far out of sight. Like *Aura,* the story is concentrated in time. Here it is merely a brief stopover of one day and night in Cholula by four (?) people on the way to Vera Cruz and the sea. But compressed within this "real" time is Fuentes's obsession with time itself, with history and reality. As Emir Rodríguez-Monegal points out, Fuentes wishes to introduce simultaneously various dimensions of time.[13] Through Javier or through the Narrator we see the same pyramid and the role it played in Cortez's time; hear invented accounts from a newspaper supposedly dating back to the Middle Ages; learn of events, of people, real and fictitious (historical accuracy is irrelevant) that have echoes in the present. Also, as we have noted in Fuentes's previous works, the theme of sacrifice is a preoccupation. This is particularly important in the handling of the characterization of witches.

Sacrifice: the Witch as Sacrificial Victim. In *Aura* and in *Where the Air Is Clear,* Fuentes's witches practiced sacrifice either to further their magic or for religious reasons. In *Aura* there is no commentary on this practice; in *Where the Air Is Clear* it is debated by the characters, some like Zamacona condemning Mexico's bloody past, others like Ixca finding it the better of two evils:

> Do you think this cheap market-place power, without any greatness, is better than a power which at least had the imagination to ally itself with the great forces, permanent and inviolable, of the cosmos? With the sun itself? I tell you I'd rather die immolated on a sacrificial stone than buried under the excrement of capitalist tricks and newspaper gossip.[14]

But in *Change of Skin* the situation is partially reversed. We see the witch not only as persecutor, but as sacrificial victim of society. Elizabeth resorts to the black arts in self-defense because she is exploited and then discarded by Javier. This is a theme that we might have predicted in Fuentes, given the concluding observations of "Mito" in *Holy Place* that the witch is also innocent.

In like manner, on a historical plane, we are given intimations of other victims of society. In the Narrator's "newspaper" we hear of innocent women accused of being witches and burned at the stake. (Fuentes's intimations here are in fact supported by Marvin Harris in *Cows, Pigs, Wars and Witches*, in which he documents the role of "witches" as scapegoats for the Inquisition, serving to deflect popular wrath away from the real oppressors in society to defenseless victims, by and large old and lower-class women.)[15]

Witches and Nazis. Fuentes's references to the burning of witches and the ovens of the Nazi concentration camps are not accidentally juxtaposed. In his intuitive approach to history he tries to suggest, I believe, that both are parts of the same phenomenon, of man's dogmatism and his assertion of the right to judge and sacrifice the outsider. It is perhaps for this reason that

Fuentes is highly sensitive to the implication by *New York Times* critic David Gallagher that he is in fact defending Nazism.[16]

But if Gallagher took the defense of Nazism to be a little too convincing, and "the clichés of the Right to be vested with greater zest than all the other clichés in the book,"[17] the fault lies largely in Fuentes's intentional ambiguity.[18] Just as Fuentes wavers in his relationship to the witch and as he is attracted and repelled by the anima, the archetype of life, he is equally fascinated, equally troubled, by all manifestations of the unconscious, whether collective or individual.

The Influence of Nietzsche. Both in his letter to the *New York Times* and in his published interview in *Insula* with José Miguel Ullán,[19] Fuentes defends and praises Nietzsche, and in *Insula* he asserts that along with Marx, Nietzsche is one of the great influences in his life. Commenting on his own characterization of the novel as "a combination of revolutionary seriousness and anarchical joy," he says:

> Yes, I hope that one can feel this tension. For me it is very important because basically it's an unresolved conflict of my own, an intellectual, schizoid acceptance, which I do not think is unusual, of both the Marxist and Nietzschean vision. . . . Let us say that in *Change of Skin* there is an implicit Marxist vision (very implicit because it has been too explicit in my other works) of what man owes to the world . . . and a Nietzschean vision of what he owes to himself.[20]

Perhaps the implicit vision in *Change of Skin* is not implicit enough to make its weight felt by readers not thoroughly familiar with Fuentes's political ideas. But the Nietzschean aspect of this work is as disturbing as it is predictable from all that we have already found in Fuentes's fascination with the theme of the witch. Fuentes states: "Revolutionary thinkers (Sade and Nietzsche included) are not sponsors of evil; they are sponsors of freedom who must courageously recognize that freedom can lead to evil, yet that the risk is worth taking."[21] Fuentes sees himself, like Nietzsche, as a voice for freedom, for antidogmatism. (Every one of Nietzsche's declarations is denied by other declarations and this, rather than proving his eclecticism, constitutes the very coherence of his work.)[22]

Yet the disturbing aspect of Nietzsche, according to the writings of Jung, is not that by speaking out freely he influenced others in a manner injurious to society, but that Nietzsche expresses eloquently and anticipates social phenomena that come into being not through his own direct influence, but because both Nietzsche's expressions and the phenomena are the expression of a collective unconscious.

Jung, in fact, like Fuentes, seems to have been very attracted by Nietzsche. Nietzsche had even anticipated Jung in the insight he brought to the study of dreams. For Nietzsche, dreams revealed an earlier, preconscious state of mankind to which we return nightly with relief after the daytime strain on our conscious forces. He wrote:

I hold that as man now still reasons in dreams, so men reasoned when awake through thousands of years . . . this ancient element in human nature still manifests itself in our dreams. . . . the dream carries us back to remote conditions of human culture and provides a ready means of understanding them better . . . like dreams, the poet and artist are also useful in that they recall an older humanity and can assist us to the understanding of it.[23]

Nevertheless, Jung warned his readers in the late thirties about this older humanity that artists like Nietzsche and ordinary, disturbed Germans were evoking in their dreams:

> Nietzsche was but one case among thousands and millions of the future Germans in whose unconsciousness the Germanic cousin of Dionysos, that is Wotan, developed during the Great War. In the dreams of Germans whom I treated then I could clearly see the Wotanistic revolution coming on. Those Germans were by no means people who had studied *Thus Spake Zarathustra,* and surely those young people who started the pagan sacrifices of sheep did not know of Nietzsche's experiences.[24]

We may compare Jung's observation with the report cited by Hill and Williams in *The Supernatural* (published in 1965, two years before *Change of Skin*) of "a Mexican cult, whose rituals (which regularly included the drinking of a powerful brew of marijuana leaves) were climaxed by human sacrifice in a cave temple." The report goes on to state that the cult had already been in existence at least six years and that members considered themselves reincarnations of such historic figures as St. Francis of Assisi.[25]

The foregoing is not meant to suggest that the actual newspaper accounts, which Fuentes may have seen, influenced the composition of *Change of Skin* any more than that the literary work influenced the young cultists, but that both are in fact modern expressions—albeit on two distinct levels—of the cult of the irrational with all the good, or evil, that this may entail in today's world.

Another commentary on the same phenomenon of the irrational, which would probably be just as disturbing to Fuentes as Gallagher's remark, is offered by Marvin Harris in his already mentioned *Cows, Pigs, Wars and Witches*. Harris asserts that "the return of the witch is not a mere inscrutable bit of whimsy. The modern witch-craft craze has definite points of similarity with the late medieval craze." The counterculture stands "shoulder to shoulder with the Inquisition on the issue of witch's flight . . . witches are once more as believable as anything else. . . . The modern witch fad blunts and befuddles the forces of dissent . . . it postpones development of a rational set of political commitments. And that is why it is so popular among the more affluent segments of our population. That is why the witch has returned."[26]

Harris's commentary on witches and other fads for the irrational in today's society can be neatly inserted into the usual Marxist criticism of Fuentes's mythological writing. As a typical bourgeois, middle-aged author, he has naturally betrayed his youthful idealism and is now trying to sidetrack revolutionary progress into the dark forests of the unconscious.

Yet Fuentes's psychological attitude is far too complex to serve as a stable target for any kind of simplistic critique. Like his hero, Nietzsche, he is a chameleon. He is constantly flirting with the irrational, reflecting its social existence in his literary work, yet failing to defend it in any definitive way. This he cannot do because it would destroy the dialectic of his own thinking. Nevertheless, it cannot be denied that although one manifestation of irrational—the cult of Nazism—is the object of his attack and condemnation, another manisfestion—the cult of monks with their new rites of modern music, ritual dancing and sex—exercises a fascination for him that is not far removed from the irrational attraction behind Nazism.

The Monks

But before analyzing the attraction of these six mysterious characters, the monks, we should attempt to define them in somewhat greater detail. In the last chapter of *Change of Skin*, they almost completely replace the original couples (although Isabel, being "unreal" herself and not even boasting any "unreal" memories, has no double among the monks). As already indicated, the treatment of the archetypal character, of woman as witch, in the first sections of the novel strongly resembles Fuentes's treatment of the same theme in his earlier works. It varies and vacillates from the subtle (Mercedes) to the obvious (Aura), but there is usually some tenuous link with reality; that is, as the term is usually understood. In the final chapter of *Change of Skin*, however, the technique of character presentation is far closer to that in *Holy Place*. Although the monks are presented as modern hippies, just as Claudia is presented as a Mexican movie star, we know that they are in reality symbols who represent myths—in other words, undisguised archetypes. And as Claudia represents Circe and other magical female incarnations, so White Rabbit can represent not only Elizabeth, but as anima she is also Helen of Troy, and the Virgin Mary (p. 417).

The Narrator indicates that the monks differ from Fuentes's earlier characters by saying that Raúl and Ophelia, Becky and Gershon, etc. lived in his house (p. 433). The monks, however, are only transient guests whom he can dispose of at will. Yet the Narrator, prey

to the schizoid frame of mind to which Fuentes himself
admitted in the Ullán interview, refuses to accept this
reality: "I refuse to admit that if I should relax my will
and imagination, the six young faces and bodies traveling
with me would be carried away into darkness. . . . that
they. . . . are my creatures and if I should cease to sustain
them with my creative love, . . . they would vanish even
from memory" (p. 423).

And yet the reader cannot be sure that the monks are
only the Narrator's brain children, for they exercise a
power of their own over him, and he fears them.

> I don't want to look at them . . . because . . . these
> sighs are those of the Medusa struggling to be born
> again . . . this litany is that of the Furies giving birth
> to rivers of blood and crops of bones . . . the six
> Monks are impregnating themselves in order to tell
> us that another history exists in which our own is
> hardly a nightmare reserved for the long sleep of
> death.[27]

(This is roughly translated in the English version as:
"Their chant goes on and I begin to tremble. *We are the
androgynous pages. We are the cherubs of innocence.
We are the spell-cast virgins* . . . . We are neither men
nor women nor good nor evil nor body nor spirit. . . .
nor consciousness nor instinct [p. 433].) The English
translation does little to resolve our dilemma in identifying the monks. Both paragraphs emphasize the negative, the mysterious, the invincible. Like the walls of
Jericho, the identity of the monks can only be approached by a circuitous route.

Their Relationship to the Narrator. Only one thing is
clear. The monks possess an entirely different relationship to the Narrator than either of the two female char-

acters to whom he addressed himself earlier. With Elizabeth he is confident; he has even interfered in her life in his role of taxi driver. With Isabel, as we have seen, he is master. But with the monks, whom he admits are emanations of his own imagination, he is afraid. He cannot control them, and in the end he goes along with them: "I didn't know how and I couldn't stop them, Dragoness. The enthusiasm of belonging won me over. And also knowing that I am going on forty. I was going to be young again with them." (p. 433, Spanish; p. 451, English).

Their youth, their vitality is contagious. Unlike the other characters who by and large remain in their role of characters with respect to the Narrator—that is, elements outside him whom he can understand and control—the monks appear to represent parts of the Narrator's psyche uncontrolled by conscious reason. Thus they loom before him now as witches, now as ghosts of tortured children of Franz's concentration camp, and again as priests, as avengers as well as victims. They go on to the end of all the old contradictions "in order to live and repeal them, ridding ourselves of our old skin and exchanging it for the fresh new skin of the new contradictions, those that will await us" (p. 441).

As witches, they remind us of Circe and her court in *Holy Place*. As in *Holy Place* one of the monks is a priest; there is dancing around a magic circle, and chanting of a litany. The Narrator brings them to a brothel which serves as a setting for a witches' sabbat with all its indiscriminate sexuality and intellectual blasphemies. From the brothel the monks are brought back to the Narrator's castle-home, a former Jesuit monastery, and the Black Mass of inversions continues. The purple-red cloak of a Catholic cardinal is given to one of the monks, a hood of black and scarlet to another. Others are propitiated with different gifts, historical remnants.

Their Adversary, the Wise Old Man, Herr Urs. The
Narrator tries to oppose the monks with conscious
thought, but his conscious mind fails him. Finally, he
can only oppose them with another emanation of the
unconscious, the toothless, smiling Jew, who sold him
the magical trunk with its gifts of the past. Fuentes does
not tell us who this old man, this wizard, is, but we can
find his ancestral form among Jung's archetypes. He is
the Wise Old Man, the archetype of meaning. He is, in
Jung's words,

> an immortal daemon that pierces the chaotic dark-
> nesses of brute life with the light of meaning. He
> is the enlightener, the master teacher, a psychopomp
> whose personification even Nietzsche, that breaker
> of tablets, could not escape—for he had called up
> his reincarnation in Zarathustra, the lofty spirit of
> an almost Homeric age, as the carrier and mouth-
> piece of his own Dionysian enlightenment and
> ecstasy.[28]

Like the anima, the wise old man is bipolar, the good
magician and the evil dwarf. "If the name Lucifer were
not prejudicial, it would be a very suitable one for this
archetype."[29] It is as evil dwarf, unfortunately, that the
wise old man archetype confronts the monks. The seller
of the trunk seems to have incarnated himself in the
puppet of Herr Urs, whom we had last seen as a corpse
in Franz's refrigerator. Now he steps out of the trunk as
"a little god, a god of the hearth, a familiar, like the
rabbits and the cats" (p. 421, Spanish; p. 438 English).
Like the hero of Nietzsche, he explains:

> I abandoned my childhood faith, in exchange for
> knowledge. And I discovered then that knowledge
> is secret, that it has two faces, one of which . . . has

been kept hidden. It is dual and diabolic like our
very universe without answer. . . . I discovered that
knowledge was above all a way of descending into
the buried world where the truth of creation is yet
to be found. . . . (pp. 438, 439).

For Franz, Herr Urs represents an unknown disease
which the dwarf explains is the disease of freedom:
"Freedom's discovery makes us ill because we have believed that subjugation is health" (p. 439). Through Herr
Urs, the archetype of meaning, knowledge leads to truth
(the truth of creation), which leads to absolute liberty.
Herr Urs turns out to be a far more formidable devil's
advocate than Brother Thomas, but the practical message
for mankind is not too different. Brother Thomas had
said, "We wished to be hated in order to be loved in-
tensely" (p. 400). And Herr Urs says, "What I ask is that
you do what can never be forgiven. Only in this case is
it worth while to humiliate yourself seeking redemp-
tion" (p. 442).

Confronted with his presence, with the words "everything is permitted" (p. 441), the sensitive White Rabbit
reacts as Jeanne Fery, the nun, in the power of the Devil
and goes into a convulsion vomiting testicles of goats
and worms. But Herr Urs is not quite the Devil. He is
even more ambitious. In a key paragraph omitted from
the English translation (on page 441), he says that he
decided to stop being God and to become the Creator:

"Then I could really be credited with the totality of
the world, not just with love, justice, death and
nothingness which are the poor attributes of God.
I wanted to be all and at the same time the unknown,
the original catastrophe that we will never recover
as a unity, but whose visions only the Creator can
evoke. I wanted to be more than that God captured

in the poor schemes of life and death." (p. 424,
Spanish)

The philosophic assumption behind Herr Urs's words
is clearly not that of Christianity. His references to the
original catastrophe and an all-powerful creator, not to
be confused with a captive god, have clear precedents
in Gnostic thought. Jung, whose interest in the unconscious also led him to study the Gnostics, tells us that
in their belief earthly life was created not by a single,
powerful being, but by a demiurge that incubated the
chaotic waters of the beginning, remaining in matter in
a potential state, and that the primary chaotic condition
has therefore persisted.[30] Also, as reflected in Herr Urs's
ideas, in Gnostic thought there is a supreme creator besides this God or demiurge that presides over our world
and is only the last emanation of the Godhead.[31]

Commenting upon Gnosticism in the present, Sydney
Herbert Mellone, author of *The New Testament and
Modern Life*, depicts it as

> a free, natural-growing religion of isolated minds,
> of separate little circles and isolated sects. It is based
> on revelation, which even at the present time is im-
> parted to the individual, upon the more or less con-
> vincing force of the religious imagination and spec-
> ulations of a few leaders, etc. Its adherents feel
> themselves to be the isolated, the few, the free and
> enlightened as opposed to the sluggish and inert
> masses of mankind.[32]

Herr Urs, who is as puppet, of course, only another
creature of the Narrator, on an intellectual plane seems
to represent the Gnostic heresy which is not at all in-
compatible with his mythical role as archetype of the

Wise Old Man or dwarf. (It should perhaps be pointed out that this archetypal figure is most typical of eastern European fairy tales, and so it is most appropriate that Herr Urs be a Czech.) Like the Gnostics and like the elusive Rumpelstiltskin, Herr Urs emphasizes his isolation: "My freedom is my isolation and my victory is to hold myself apart, identifying with no one and with nothing. . . ." (p. 440). But his reasoning is devious. Although isolated himself, he contaminates others. Although his personal system of values may be Gnostic or Nietzschean or be called by any other philosophical or religious term we care to use, his social role is negative. It is to unite "all that is solitary, brutal, indifferent or corrupt" in each one of us with that which is the same in him, in others (p. 425, Spanish; missing on p. 433, English). It is his sickness, his kind of liberty that has infected not only Franz, but every potential Franz. He identifies with no one, but he organizes isolation, is always on the side of Caesar. He compares himself to a "dark star," a "distant contamination" (p. 440).[33]

Thus the dwarf, the wise old man, although he first appears as if to rescue the Narrator from the unconscious, betrays the trust. The archetype of meaning can be as dangerous as the anima, the archetype of life. The search for meaning or knowledge leads man to the truth of the mysteries of creation and, once liberated by this truth, there are no moral laws to restrain him.

In his role of archetype, therefore, Herr Urs hammers home the message that the Narrator had tried to preach in the earlier episode of the brothel:

Truth bares its teeth at us from every side. The danger is not the lie; it is truth which waits to put us to sleep . . . and to impose itself as at the very beginning. If we were to let it, truth would annihilate

life. Because truth is the same as the beginning and
the beginning is nothingness . . . The apocalypse is
the other face of creation (p. 422).

The literary lie[34] betrays the truth in order to postpone
the day of judgment in which the beginning and the end
will be one.[35]

Thus the Narrator, far from being the powerful deus
ex machina that he appears to be in the greater part of
the work, in the final section is menaced from all sides—
by the "collective violence" implicit in truth, in meaning, and by the "individual violence" of life itself
(p. 442). His choice of the latter, his decision to follow
the monks and do nothing to prevent the execution of
Franz, is a choice between two evils. Forced to choose
between witches and Nazis, he reluctantly accepts the
witches, puts the dwarf back in his suitcase.[36] But he
does this fully aware that the monks have contracted the
disease they wanted to cure (p. 431). The condemnation
of Franz is implicitly compared to that of Jesus: "Jacob
Werner, born in the year zero, condemns to death Franz
born 2000 years ago" (p. 449). A new religious era is
initiated. Like the Nazis, the monks are explicitly anti-
Christian. But theirs is a paganism of the oppressed
rather than of the oppressors; they are the children of
the Nazi's victims. Yet the cycle of revenge must continue. Even the semblance of justice in revenge is not
important.

The Narrator wants to remind them of their own max-
ims, that each one of us is, in one way or another, guilty
of every sin that any one of us has committed (p. 449).
In the final analysis, Franz is condemned not because
of his guilt but because he stands for the old, and he
must die (p. 451). This is the pattern of life. Yet the
"new" monks are already contaminated by the old. In
their verdict for retribution they perpetuate the age-old

violence they are condemning, renew the cycle of victim
and oppressor which travels, propelled by blood, through
history. The Nazis and the witches, in playing their pre-
destined roles, assure each other's death and survival.

The constant reassertion of old forms is also echoed
in the original theme of Javier and Elizabeth. With Franz
dead and Isabel on her way to Mexico City, the original
couple come together again and renew their old struggle
of love and hate without which they cannot live. On the
practical plane of the drama between husband and wife,
and on the psychological plane of the drama in the Narrator's mind, the solution is the same. Old patterns must
continue; the apparently new is only the old in another
form. As the yellowed pages of Javier's manuscript say,
"Each man born is a first creation. He must repeat everything for himself and for the world . . . as if nothing had
ever happened before his birth" (p. 448).

The major theme of *Change of Skin*, therefore, is the
same as that of *Aura* and *Holy Place* and even of his
earlier excursion into the subject, "Tlactocatzine." Woman
is treated as life itself, as destiny—whether she is witch,
or ghost, or some other manifestation of the anima.

In *Aura* the hero makes no real attempt to escape her.
In *Holy Place* the hero, no less fascinated by her, nevertheless struggles to overcome her by magic, by in fact
becoming her. And he fails. In *Change of Skin* there
again appears to be a choice between acceptance or rejection. But it turns out not to be the choice of free will
versus predestination. Man (Javier or the Narrator) must
choose between two symbols of the unconscious: Javier,
between two witches—Elizabeth, the witch of the old,
and Isabel, the witch of the new; the Narrator, between
the diabolical dream of knowledge, of finding the truth
behind the universe, or of accepting the dream of life
as he finds it—irrational, ignorant, forever condemning
itself to reaffirmation and repetition of old forms. Per-

haps the vision of man's fate does not grow more pessimistic between *Aura* and *Change of Skin,* but the direct, emotional approach in Fuentes's early handling of the theme now has all the weight of the intellect added to it.

Author and Narrator

Although assuredly one should not make the mistake of confusing the writer with his characters (an error of which Fuentes accuses his critic in the already cited letter to the *New York Times*), there are many similarities between Fuentes and the Narrator of *Change of Skin.*

Fuentes's Characterizations of the Narrator. Playfully, Fuentes in fact hints at the physical identity between himself and the Narrator by telling us that the latter is almost forty, wears a moustache, and is a Mexican writer who lives in San Angel. But more important than these physical details is the Ullán interview with Fuentes in which the author does in fact identify with the philosphy of the Narrator. Speaking of the profound influence of Nietzsche on his thought, of the already referred to "schizophrenic intellectual adherence. . . . to the Marxist vision and to the Nietzschean vision," Fuentes says that he finds the final incarnation "of Nietzschean exaltation in *Louis Lambert* by Balzac, a novel I love as few others," a novel in which

> "the willful contamination makes possible the disappearance of the bridge between subject and predicate . . . the open space means the possibility itself of contamination. Lambert, like Nietzsche, like the narrator in *Change of Skin,* will be locked into a prison-hospital-insane asylum-church because he is

an open, dangerous being. You'll soon see that there is a reason why my narrator is called [Freddy Lambert]."[37]

Lambert, the mystical hero of one of Balzac's early novels, is also one of Fuentes's heroes, and of course Fuentes identifies with him. In Freddy[38] Lambert, Fuentes has created a narrator to echo his own philosophy, one who mirrors his own contagion by intellectual and emotional forces often pulling in opposite directions. David Gallagher says of the Narrator, of Freddy Lambert, "He underlines the fact that the entire action of the novel is an apocryphal game conducted in his own mind, which is, of course, a figment of Fuentes's."[39]

But Fuentes displays considerable mischievous skill in other characterizations of his Narrator. In his interview with Rodríguez-Monegal, Fuentes suggests that the Narrator could be any of the characters[40] (but since all of them are his brainchildren in varying degrees of disguise, the statement does not add to our knowledge of this elusive character). At another point in the same interview he says, "the novelist would like to be the twin of Satan, the curious one, the tempter, the condemned one."[41] Here he seems to be using the words "novelista" and "narrador" interchangeably for this is, in fact, the role played by the Narrator, "the twin of Lucifer, the curious one, the tempter, the condemned."

The Narrator's Precedent in Ixca Cienfuegos. However, if we were to study the role of Narrator as character, instead of as Narrator, instead of deus ex machina, we would indeed find that he is a kind of devil or wizard, the natural offspring of another wizard in Fuentes. More than Louis Lambert, he reminds one of Ixca Cienfuegos. Ixca, too, inspired amazing and fantastically detailed confidences on the part of all the other characters of

Where the Air Is Clear. His mere presence seemed to be enough to elicit memories, confessions, emotional and intellectual revelations. Like Ixca, too, he seduces his heroine. In his role as taxi driver he speaks to Javier (who was about to go home with his wife and make love to her), and frustrates their passion. Elizabeth says "the taxi driver spoiled everything. I will never remember what he said. But he destroyed me" (p. 244). And the Narrator himself says:

> "That was what you told me that evening, Dragoness. I remember well. I had seen it that night in your apartment with Javier passed out in the living room . . . . If you cooled down, I didn't notice it, word of honor." (p. 245)

Ixca, who is "half real, half spirit, partly witness, partly active character,"[42] has been extensively studied by Joseph Sommers in his *After the Storm.* As Sommers points out, Ixca supports the structure of the earlier novel, acts almost like a psychoanalyst in bringing men face to face with their unconscious, reveals the denied qualities that tie them to the past. Ixca, says Sommers, "is partially a descendent of the Plumed Serpent of Lawrence." But in Fuentes's view the longing of Ixca to return to the past is not regenerative (as it was for Lawrence); "its fatalism and hostility must be accounted for, but its portent is essentially tragic." Thus, "he has developed Ixca within an author-character relationship of distance rather than identification."[42]

Although Ixca and Freddy Lambert have much in common, therefore, there is a significant difference between them. Ixca did not have the stage to himself. He was opposed by Manuel Zamacona with his frustrated message of hope and change, of the future instead of the past.

But Freddy has no other character to oppose him. He is producer, director, and even leading actor. The only debates are those within his own mind. As we have seen, he does not accept Nazism (he calls the Aztecs "Fascists"), but neither does he close his mind to it. His attitude is ambiguous enough for Gallagher to assert that "he appears to wish that the energies of the enchained animal [the Mexican tiger that has been artificially tamed] be authentically unleashed."[43] This, in Fuentes's mind, is certainly untrue, as his already cited reply to Gallagher demonstrates. His own point of view may be best summed up in another remark by the Narrator that the literary lie "pays homage to original might, unacceptable, mortal force. If we did not recognize it, not limit it, we would open the doors wide for the beast to escape in all its murderous purity" (p. 422).

This is also the point of view of Jung, who deals with the unconscious not because he wishes to unleash the energies of the chained animal, but rather to make us aware of its power, so that we may understand it better and protect ourselves.[44] Nevertheless, Fuentes pays far greater homage to the unconscious in *Change of Skin* than he does in *Where the Air Is Clear*. The author-character relationship of distance with Ixca becomes one of identification with Freddy, who is "Satan, the curious one, the temptor." There is undoubtedly a purely literary explanation for this difference (the distinct conception of the two works and their inspiration in the works of separate authors).[45] Yet there is also an unescapable psychological conclusion that in the ten years between the publication of *Where the Air Is Clear* and *Change of Skin*, Fuentes found increasing justification for paying homage to brute force, for expressing and exorcising his pessimistic view of human nature. Criticism of Fuentes because of his concern with the unconscious, the irrational element in human nature, is probably based on a misunderstanding of his intent. Yet given the ambiguous presentation of his "message," Fuentes does in fact expose himself to attacks of this kind. There is, however, another kind of criticism directed against Fuentes which, in my opinion, is altogether justifiable. This is his excessive intellectualism, which in the case of *Change of Skin* Gallagher labels "dubious, hipster-existentialist, sub-Mailerish philosophy," or "undergraduate variations on Nietzsche."[46]

Such a description represents an unjustifiably low evaluation of Fuentes as a philosopher, but it is an altogether natural and human reaction to the narrator's constant preaching, his antidogmatic dogmatism which turns out to be as distasteful as the object of its attack.

Intellectualism and Archetypes

The overdose of intellectualism which we find in Fuentes's recent novels is certainly open to criticism. It is, however, the rule rather than the exception in the contemporary Latin American novel. The critic Raúl H. Castagnino describes this general tendency as "excessive intellectualization which can lead to an asphyxiating dehumanization or—as in decadent baroque mannerisms—a game of wits or puzzles."[47]

In my own view, the intellectual novel in which the intellectualizing represents the point of view of the author (and not a development of character as is the case, for example, in Dostoevski) runs the risk of degenerating into an essay. It is a development which tends to antagonize the reader who anticipates the escapism of the more conventional novel. Furthermore, if this essay is combined with an abstruse fairy tale whose avowed object is to confuse rather than to enlighten, the reader is likely to give up in desperation. The chief objection I have to Fuentes's witches and wizards is that they are too easily recognizable as his brainchildren.

Even Teódula Moctezuma, the witch based on a real prototype, is given an archetypal presentation. We are told no details of character unrelated to her archetypal nature. We never see her as an ordinary old woman, for example, with an old woman's problems. Every detail concerning Teódula must point to the fact that she is a witch and a symbol of Mexico's Aztec past. Of all of Fuentes's leading witches (here I exclude such interesting, but roughly sketched, minor witches as Mercedes and Ludivinia), Elizabeth of *Change of Skin* is the only one who manages to free herself sufficiently from the author to lead some sort of independent existence, even if it is only an existence of the imagination. Only in Elizabeth has Fuentes realized his twin goal (first mentioned in his interview in *Siempre*, p. 15) to both "mythify and personalize." In the case of the other witches, he has largely sacrificed personality to mythology (although there are also some very real, nonmythological details about Claudia). But it is perhaps partially due to these very complexities in Elizabeth that the mythical theme of *Change of Skin* appears more abstruse than in the other novels, and that the author has felt the need to depend so heavily upon the intellectual commentaries of the Narrator.

According to Raúl Castagnino, this increasing intellectualism to which Fuentes and his Latin American fellow novelists have fallen prey is a dangerous tendency. He concludes that "just as in this fashion poetry has led to anti-poetry, and theatre has become anti-theatre [theatre of the absurd?], so the contemporary Spanish-American novel is coming close to being an anti-novel."[48] Yet in Fuentes's own thinking, his recent work does not constitute a conscious attack on the novelistic form. He maintains that "what I am writing cannot be said, cannot

be expressed, in any way except through novels . . . ."[49]
But he does not defend techniques used in his last novels
by any yardstick of reality. He admits, for example, that
the relationship between Javier and Elizabeth is a kind
of "dialogue of mirrors," and protests that the only way
to understand *Change of Skin* is to accept its absolute
fictionality. "It never attempts to be a reflection of reality. It attempts to be a revolutionary kind of fiction, carried to its logical consequences."[50]

A *Broader Literary Perspective on Fuentes.* The literary precedents for Fuentes's absolute fiction may be
suggested by several of the general ideas developed by
Northrop Frye in his *Anatomy of Criticism.* Frye says
that "the study of archetypes is the study of literary symbols as parts of a whole, and this forces us to conceive
the possibility of a self-contained literary universe."[51]
This universe is "no longer a commentary on life or
reality, but [contains] life and reality in a system of verbal relationships."[52] In the literary universe everything
is potentially identical to everything else. The literary,
poetic world is an apocalyptic one, but although it reveals, it does so only on its own terms. When poets or
writers enter this final phase of self-expression, "they
enter a phase of which only religion, or something as
infinite as religion, can possibly form an external goal . . .
because the transcendental and apocalyptic perspective
of religion comes as a tremendous emancipation of the
imaginative mind."[53] The use of archetypes, therefore,
ultimately implies a religious goal, broadly interpreted,
and since "the structural principles of literature are as
closely related to mythology and comparative religion
as those of painting are to geometry," the symbolism of
the Bible (and to a lesser extent of classical mythology)
is considered a grammar of literary archetypes.[54] Thus
Frye regards today's apparently revolutionary literary

forms not as a passing intellectual phase, but as a modern expression of art forms that go back to the Middle Ages and beyond.

The Archetypal Masque. Of particular interest for our purposes in understanding *Change of Skin* are Frye's commentaries about the archetypal masque—the modern form of sophisticated drama which he shows is based on the antimasque, which predates the morality play and is the most primitive of all dramatic forms. If we consider only the last chapter of *Change of Skin*, it is in fact a masque involving demonic and supernatural figures. One of the characters, faceless White Rabbit, changes her mask several times, enacting new roles. The setting is symbolic (the former Jesuit monastery and the house of prostitution), and we know the characters only as actors. They appear and disappear out of nowhere. In the most concentrated form of the archetypal masque, according to Frye, the action takes place inside the human mind—as it does in *Change of Skin*. This is explicit in the old morality plays and implicit in Maeterlinck, Pirandello, Andreyev, and Strindberg.[55]

These plays are characterized by a sense of confusion and fear, and the constant undermining of the distinction between illusion and reality "as mental projections become physical bodies and vice versa, [splitting] the action up into a kaleidoscopic chaos of reflecting mirrors."[56] (We may remember that the same image of reflecting mirrors was used by Fuentes to describe the relationship between Elizabeth and Javier.)

Of the many examples of the archetypal masque that Frye discusses, the most interesting for our purposes is Andreyev's *The Black Maskers*, because of its fusion of personal and social themes. In this play, "the author saw reflected not only the destruction of the individual's *nobile castello*, which is its explicit theme, but also the

whole social collapse of modern Russia."[57] (We know
that Fuentes, like Andreyev, often identifies his narrator's individual fate with the national experience.) To
continue the analogy between the two works, we are
told that:

> [Andreyev] distinguishes two groups of dissociative
> elements of personality, one group connected with
> self-accusation and the other with the death-wish,
> and [he] exhibits the human soul as a castle pos-
> sessed by a legion of demons ... a revel of satyrs
> who have got out of control.[58]

Frye's commentaries on Andreyev seem to be made
to order for *Change of Skin*. From the viewpoint of literary history, they help to situate such a puzzling work
within a literary background and to relate it to similar
forms that have already appeared in Europe (just as Castagnino's study helps us to relate Fuentes to his like-
minded colleagues in Latin America). But it is interesting that in order to *explain* these archetypal masques,
Frye is forced to look beyond the Bible and in fact suggests the works of Jung "whose understanding of the
archetype as an aspect of personality capable of dramatic
projection ... throw[s] a great deal of light on the characterization of modern allegorical, psychic and expres-
sionist dramas, with their circus barkers and wraith-like
females and inscrutable sages and obsessed demons."[59]
Thus Frye, who had previously regarded Jung with
mixed feelings[60] as an aid in literary interpretation, is
finally forced to make use of the Jungian key to unlock
these highly complex literary symbols. Although Jung's
point of departure lay in dreams more than in literature,
his interpretations were obviously applicable to the
world of literature which we might describe as one of
"printed dreams." Similarly, although Frye deals basi-

cally with European (and American) poetry and drama, his commentaries about current literary tendencies are obviously applicable to Fuentes's novels, which reveal strong influences of both modern poetry and theatre.

In the preceding pages, we have depended heavily on Jung to explain the probably psychological (and at times philosophical) meaning of Fuentes's more obscure scenes involving magical characters. Through Frye, we can situate Fuentes's often disturbing techniques within an established literary framework. Thus Fuentes's witches and wizards are recognized as the product of psychological, philosophical, and literary premises.

As readers, we may be critical of the witch and wish that Fuentes would create a more believable or more personal image in his female characters. But as literary critics we cannot deny that Fuentes's witch, whether she is called Aura or Claudia or Elizabeth, plays an integral role in his total concept of the universe, and so long as his work retains its highly philosophical orientation, he probably cannot get along without her.

V
Cumpleaños (Birthday): The Witch as Goddess*

In 1969, two years after Fuentes's publication of *Change of Skin*, I received a copy of his next novel, *Cumpleaños* (*Birthday*, a novel which, to my knowledge, has not been translated into English), with an inscription from the author: "more witches!" Consciously, now without question, Fuentes was still possessed by the anima figure. Furthermore, as Jung's observations had suggested, in the process of refinement and elaboration, the magical female had now been reduced by Fuentes to a pure essence.

As we have already observed, Elizabeth of *Change of Skin* had been multifaceted, subject to human weaknesses, almost equally believable as woman as in her role of witch. But Nuncia of *Cumpleaños*, although succeeding Elizabeth in the chronological order of Fuentes's publications, is far closer to Aura. In fact, she seems to be a shadow of Aura. Rather than the portrait of a woman, she is a figure in a landscape. But the landscape is an interior one, a subterranean cave-like structure with

*"Parts of this chapter originally appeared in *Latin American Literary Review* 2, no. 4, Spring-Summer 1974, with the title '*Cumpleaños*, a Mythological Interpretation of an Ambiguous Novel.'"

thick drapery, all the symbolic imagery of the uterus. Nuncia lives in a labyrinth whose only other inhabitants are a boy and a cat.

The narrator of the tale, an English architect, a run-of-the-mill man who has been thinking only of his son's tenth birthday, cannot explain his sudden presence in the labyrinth. At first even Nuncia does not acknowledge his presence. But he is attracted to the woman just as he is repelled by the obvious malevolence of the child. Unwillingly, however, he is forced into a blood pact of eternal companionship with the evil child, who then disappears.

In the following scene the narrator is already Nuncia's lover. The subterranean world opens out into a magical park, but the idyllic relationship between the lovers comes to sudden end with the appearance of a horseman identical to the narrator, a character who is, in fact, a different version of the narrator and who insists upon sharing Nuncia. The narrator's attempt to kill his double (who turns out to be the diabolical child) fails, and the horseman metamorphoses into Siger of Brabante, a thirteenth-century Averroist philosopher. According to Nuncia, Siger is the reincarnation of Christ and is also her very own child. But to Siger and all his previous incarnations—the narrator himself being only a possible future incarnation of the same character—Nuncia is a liar and a madwoman. Thus, as in the Japanese novel *Rashomon*, we have conflicting versions of the identies and facts in the case. The reader is forced to investigate the details, to examine the characters of the two witnesses with all the insight at his or her command.

Let us first concern ourselves with Nuncia. Her constant companion, the cat, is a suspicious element. (Cats are frequently used as "familiars" by witches; that is, they aid in the conjuring up of magical powers.)[1] Nuncia uses herbs and keeps cages of animals on the premises, both occupations traditionally pursued by the witch. She is of indeterminate age, of ambiguous beauty. She is painted in the classic colors of the Earth Mother (colors always associated with death and blood scarifice): her robes are black, her hair is red. Her deathly pallor of complexion (which is compared to a dying star, p. 19)[2] and the presence of large numbers of keys in her pockets (p. 18) are further details identifying her with Hecate, goddess of the moon and mother of witches who "as mistress of the way down and of the lower way . . . has for her symbols the key, the phallic opening power of the male, the emblem of the Goddess who is mistress of birth and conception."[4]

Although there is little doubt that Nuncia is a witch, the question nevertheless arises as to what kind of witch she may be. Is the force she exerts positive or negative? By her own account she is the Virgin herself, Mother of God. If she really is, this would indicate that Fuentes's attitude toward the witch has done an about-face since the days of Teódula Moctezuma, the distinctly negative character in *Where the Air is Clear* (1958), who was a willing henchwoman of the ancient powers. Nuncia supposedly not only refuses to pay homage to the devil, she actively opposes him. But if she is the Virgin Mary, she is far from typical of the orthodox figure. Here the Holy Ghost is seen as "the diabolical multiplicity" (p. 51), and the new twist is that the Virgin Mary rebels at giving birth to the son of the monster:

> "I learned that I was that vessel, that intolerable unit of evil disguised as its opposite. My fetus, engendered by diabolical multiplicity, found in me the container of its unity. I could not tolerate this wisdom." (p. 51)

The Witch as Gnostic Virgin

Though Nuncia may be the Virgin Mary, she is a Virgin who has been converted to Gnosticism. Perhaps she is the Great Mother who plays so important a role in all Gnostic systems, the Sophia who is goddess of the heavens and famous for her wisdom. She has the wisdom—and the presumption—to question the very role of God: "Why did God, who is absolute unity, have this temptation to negate himself procreating, proliferating, multiplying, those attributes which once exiled from the unity would necessarily oppose it?" (p. 52).

And so to cheat the Devil's child of his divine origin by ceasing to be a virgin, she offers herself to the old and wise Chinese merchant who confirms her suspicions with respect to the diabolical nature of her unborn child. Yet the death of her son on the cross comes to constitute the victory of the Devil: "The new religion was founded upon the dispersion of the unity; since then God ceased to be one and now we are three . . ." (p. 55). She is left with her immortal son, offspring of demonic forces, to reenact their love-hate drama throughout eternity, throughout countless reincarnations in which she alternately plays the part of mother and mistress in a relationship whose precedents we can trace back at least as far as Hesiod's *Theogony*. Kerényi comments on the birth of Aphrodite (as Hesiod relates it) that "begetting and birth are identical, as also the begetter and the begotten. The phallus is the child, and the child . . . an eternal stimulus to further procreation."[4]

But all of this is Nuncia's version of her life. It is not the son's, not Siger's. For Siger, Nuncia is only a demented servant who has been exposed to his sadistic experiments: "I obliged her to seek bestial copulation in the mountains. I mixed my semen with that of the male goat and the tigers" (p. 102). It would be little

wonder, then, if she visualized the Devil as "the hy-
bridization of the tiger, the owl, the bear, the dragon and
the goat" (p. 51). But if this is true, what manner of man
is Siger, or is he in fact either God or Devil?

Siger as Shadow

There are at least two approaches by which we can identify Siger. The first is by recourse to the clues provided
in the novel. Siger first appears at the moment when the
narrator attempts to kill his double, the horseman—symbol (as we shall discuss shortly) of the other self, the
shadow, the personal unconscious, which Jung calls "the
inferior side of the personality."[5] The narrator relates:
"I threw myself on him. I embraced a man who looked
at me with compassion, affection, and yet a certain disdain; the faded gold of his hair was an incipient white
silk" (p. 88). By an act of the narrator's will or through
the intervention of the demonic force of his pet tiger,
the unconscious self has suddenly been absorbed into
the person of an old man, Siger of Brabante. Yet it is not
only the narrator's unconscious self that Siger now holds
within himself. After recounting his endless reincarnations, he says to George, the narrator: "Now I am you"
(p. 104).

Siger as "Self"

Siger, therefore, may well be interpreted as a symbol of
wholeness as he contains all the previous male characters of the story. This viewpoint can be substantiated by
Nuncia's final remark: "He was a complete man. He was
all love: woman, men, children, lamb, wine, olives, fish.
He committed every transgression, in his eyes shone the

ambitious cruelty of an oriental despot . . ." (p. 114).
How can we reconcile this description, which stresses
his cruelty, with the repeated assertion that in one of his
reincarnations Siger was also Jesus? Why does Siger so
persistently deny any kinship or identity with Christ?
The second question is perhaps the more easily answered in that Jesus himself was highly ambiguous as
to his paternity, frequently maintaining that he was the
son of man (not God). In fact, given Siger's Gnostic train
of thought ("The first thing that we know is that the
world does not want us . . . . The fundamental error is
always the same: to dominate what does not need us, to
infuse our time in a time that is our opponent." [p. 97]),
it is little wonder that he rejects any relationship to God.
His very denial, therefore, should increase our suspicions. And finally, his words are belied if we adopt a
Jungian approach in order to understand his identity
more fully. "Christ as a hero and God-man," according
to Jung, "constitutes psychologically the archetype of
the self," which he considers to be the most central and
important of all archetypes. "The archetype of the self
has, functionally, the significance of a ruler of the inner
world, i.e. the collective unconscious."[6] We may recall
Siger's dictum: "If the human species possesses a common intelligence, the individual soul is not immortal,
but the genus of man is" (p. 94).

To return to Jung: "The self is a symbol of wholeness
. . . and therefore contains light and darkness simultaneously. In the Christ figure the opposites which are
united in the archetype are polarized into the 'light' (i.e.
'bright, clear') son of God on the one hand and the Devil
on the other . . . Christ and the dragon of the Antichrist
lie very close together as far as their historical development and cosmic significance are concerned."[7]

If we combine the clues provided by Nuncia and Siger
himself with the insight afforded by Jung, Siger actually
does clearly emerge as a Christ figure. For the same

reasons he may also be considered as the figure known to the Gnostic systems as "Primal Man," "the man who existed before the world . . . the prophet who goes through the world in various forms . . . the divine power which descends into the darkness of the material world and with whose descent begins the great drama of the world's development."[8]

But, no matter how we regard Siger, in *Cumpleaños* he is the eternally reincarnating male (in none of his previous existences has he been a woman) with a frenzy to live, to experience, to exercise his imagination along every possible route until he achieves an ecstasy of intellectual thought (an Aristotelian, Nietzschean, at times Bergsonian confluence of ideas) very similar to the final madness of the narrator in *Change of Skin*. In pursuit of this immortality Siger is dependent upon Nuncia, dependent as both husband and son. When he is a child, she cares for him; when an old man, she nurses him; when mature, she is his mistress. Though perhaps insane and slovenly (always dirtying his house with her muddy slippers, a symbol of the earth), she is still his world, his goddess. Long past infancy, he sucks at her breast. Although some readers may take this as a manifestation of depravity or a Rulfean influence, it is perhaps another manifestation of the Egyptian idea that man could drink immortality by sucking at the breast of a goddess. Heracles, for example, became immortal after a single sip from the breast of Hera.[9]

Nuncia as *Kore*

Yet Nuncia, whether we regard her as victim of Siger or of a diabolical Holy Spirit, resents her role as vessel of life, and in the first part of the novel assumes the role of a Gnostic Virgin. We may remember that she is accused by the child of emptying his cages, which we later realize contain in their entirety the "Holy Ghost"—that is, the owl, tiger, goat, dragon, and bear, the creatures whose convergence was necessary to produce the miraculous child. Raped, embittered, she tries to disperse these generative forces and to render them harmless. In the early part of the novel she reenacts the role of Persephone (or *Kore*), who was raped by the Prince of Darkness and condemned to spend a third of the year in the underworld. As *Kore*, Nuncia exemplifies equally the Greek idea of nonbeing and the Gnostic belief that propagation is a sinful dispersal of the divine spark and is essentially negative. In the first part of the book, she can rightfully be called a goddess of nonbeing. Her underworld is the condemned, enclosed house or subterranean city of the winter months. But in spring Nuncia, like Persephone, emerges to the surface again, changes her robes and loses herself in love and nature. Here we have the idyllic relationship between Nuncia and the narrator. We see her as the mature goddess of love who—with the arrival of the horseman—predictably metamorphoses once more, this time into the harlot, changing now into a low-cut gown of red taffeta (p. 63). And finally with the reenactment of the death scene of Siger about to take place, she changes costumes again, replacing the red of passion with a long white dress, white stockings and slippers (p. 90). Here she can be none other than Hecate or Diana, often equivalent names in ancient literature for the goddess of the moon and of the hunt. Her role of huntress, in fact, is made explicit in the words of the dying Siger: "The old man managed to look at the cages . . . he managed to say to Nuncia. . . . You failed to fill them up, woman, you haven't got two of the preys; you didn't succeed in hunting them all . . ." (p. 108). Gradually we see that the tiger, the owl, and the goat had been recaptured, yet the dragon and the bear were still lacking. In the final scene, still with her oriental "pallor," her hands shining "like a dying star," still Hecate or

Diana, Nuncia approaches the bear cage at a zoo. And with her magic deck of cards, she conjures up the demonic spirit in order that she may again give birth: "She was casting on the ground five worn-out cards, ancient ones: I saw their faces fall: the owl, the tiger, the goat, the bear and the dragon" (p. 113).

The Witch as Demeter, Earth Mother

In all of this, Nuncia is typical of the mythological Persephone-Demeter. Like her classical predecessor, like all manifestations of the anima, Nuncia is multifaceted. In ancient Acadia, Hera had three forms: maiden, fulfilled woman, and woman of sorrows. Similarly Hecate, Persephone, and Demeter were considered an unfolding of the same being.[10] More than to Persephone or Hecate, in fact, Nuncia seems to belong to Demeter, the Earth Mother phase of the goddess's existence. "To enter into the figure of Demeter," says Kerenyi, "means to be pursued, to be robbed, raped, to fail to understand, to rage and grieve, but then to get everything back and be born again."[11] And this happens to Nuncia, raped by the Holy Ghost, seeking understanding through the Chinese merchant, raging against the dispersal of God in the universe, grieving that she should be the tool of evil, but then getting everything back with love, giving birth again to herself and her lover. The figure of Demeter, in fact, helps to explain not only the character of Nuncia but also the very structure of the novel.

The Ever-present Element of Sacrifice

It has already been pointed out that *Cumpleaños* takes place in a labyrinth, an underworld which fluctuates between city and a single dwelling. The time is a birth-

day celebration, a fiesta, a ritual. It is the birthday of the
narrator's son; a gift must be given (in other words, the
bourgeois counterpart of an original sacrifice). The narrator at first struggles to find his way out of the labyrinth:
"The nearness of memory impelled me to leave there.
To return. I told him that I should return" (p. 16). He
questions, "How had I gotten there?" and is told by the
child, "A serious accident, a very serious accident" (p.
16). If we add to these remarks the narrator's thought
that "only a postulate of catastrophic nature could, perhaps, explain our presence here together" (p. 16), or the
child's assurance that "your family will be properly no-
tified" (p. 19), we must come to the conclusion that *Cumpleaños* takes place in the underworld of death. The
sacrifice (of his life) has been given (in a serious accident). *Cumpleaños*, therefore, must deal either with
death itself or with the dream or ritual of death. Since
the narrator never really awakens (Nuncia appears in the
very last scene of the novel), any of these suppositions
are possible.

From the moment we read the title of the story we
know that *Cumpleaños* revolves around a birthday. But
is there not more than one birthday involved? In addition to his "deathday," may this not also be the birthday
of George, the narrator himself, who is about to emerge
from the womb of Nuncia in order to reenact the old
love between herself and Siger? Or is there still another
possible explanation?

Significance of the Labyrinth

A labyrinth, we are told by psychologists like Jung and
Freud and by students of comparative religion like Mircea Eliade, is a symbol of the womb. Erich Neumann
points out that whether described in the Egyptian or

Tibetan books of the dead, or in the mystery cults of the
Greeks or the Gnostics, labyrinths are an important element in all ritual initiations. Whenever we encounter
the labyrinth, we are dealing with death and rebirth relating either to a life after death or to the mysteries of
initiation.[12] According to the same source, the labyrinth
is almost always connected with a cave or darkened
structure, and the presiding personage is always a
woman. Walking or dancing, the dead must pass through
the intricate, devouring labyrinth. It makes little difference which culture or mythology we are dealing with:
in the initiation practices of Liberia and Sierra Leone,
the members are supposed to be swallowed up by a
female monster, to remain in her womb for four years
and then to be born again;[13] in Indonesia, participants
in the initiation rite must pass through a labyrinth pre-
sided over by the queen of the underworld, in order to
be ordained to human existence again.[14] In all cases the
initiant endeavors to face death without really dying, to
descend to the realm of night and the dead and to return
alive.

It is not a mere coincidence, therefore, that many elements of *Cumpleaños* duplicate the myth of Demeter
and the Eleusinian initiation ceremonies, among the
best known in the Western world of rituals that are fun-
damentally alike the world over. Kerenyi says of the
Eleusinian ceremonies that it was necessary "to enter
into the figure of Demeter,"[15] and shows that there is
historical evidence to prove that initiants regarded themselves as goddesses, not gods. The emperor Gallienus,
for example, is called by the feminine "Galliena Au-
gusta" on certain Roman coins because of his having
been initiated into the mysteries of Eleusis.[16]

Let us refer again to the words of the narrator: "And
I, the man who acts in order that the summer, the woman
and the forest be as one with me, disappear little by little

in order to unite with them; I cease to be myself so that I may be more completely myself, I cease to be I in order to be them. . . . I don't believe . . . that I possessed Nuncia: I was Nuncia . . ." (p. 60).

Even certain details in *Cumpleaños*, at first sight meaningless, make perfect sense in terms of the initiation ceremony. We are told, for example, by Kerényi that initiates had to fast before they could hope to enter into the figure of Demeter. Only by reference to this can we explain George's embarrassment, shame, and fear at confessing that he was both hungry and thirsty: "How to tell them that I am hungry and thirsty. An unconquerable shame prevents me from doing it. It would be to admit something that I should not admit. It would be a catastrophe" (p. 20).

Also, in the early part of the Greek initiation ceremony—as in the first encounter of George with his new environment—the initiant was supposed to wander sorrowfully through the labyrinth to symbolize the early wandering of Demeter in search of her daughter. This was followed in the myth by the sacred marriage between Demeter herself and Zeus which led to the birth of the terrible but divine Brimos, the eternal being.[17] Similarly, in *Cumpleaños* there is the sacred marriage (George, becoming Nuncia, must somehow experience her rape by the "Holy Ghost") and the birth of the terrible and eternal being (malevolent child-horseman-Siger-himself).

To continue with the myth of Demeter, it is only after the rape by Zeus that Demeter finds her daughter (Persephone, or a new version of herself), and subjectively understands her own continuity and the continued existence of all living things.[18] And in *Cumpleaños* George, by the end of the novel, seems to have reached so deep a subjective understanding of his own continuity that he no longer needs the interpretation by Nuncia of what had at first been the mystery language of the initiation (the strange tongue spoken by Siger). Instinctively, George understands its mystery. Thus the myth of Persephone-Demeter and her fearful child helps to explain not only the character of Nuncia but also the odyssey of George, whether it be in fact an odyssey through the underworld of death, or perhaps only a dreamed initiation rite. It is either by intuitive knowledge of the world of myths, or by reference to the words of such scientific "mythologists" as Jung and Kerényi ("the myth as itself plus all the commentaries it has provoked," in the words of Fuentes's letter of 24 July 1969), that the mysteries and the ambiguous symbols in the work can be understood. By and large I have confined myself to the investigation of the two leading archetypes in the novel, the anima, Nuncia, and the child-hero or God, Siger. (Since Fuentes is an intellectual, his hero is obviously an intellectual hero.) But apart from these, there are many other archetypes whose identification, in some cases made instinctively by the reader, promotes the understanding of the work. One of these, of course, is the double which Jung calls "the shadow," and whom he identifies by reference to the dreams and psychotic fantasies of his patients as "the personal unconscious." But why does he turn out to be a horseman in *Cumpleaños;* why must he arrive on horseback? Again, Jung provides the insight.

The Shadow as Horseman

The horse is a symbol of the animal component in man, and very frequently dreams and mythology connect it with the Devil, either as one physical body or as the Devil's beast. The horse symbol in children's dreams inspires fear and betrays dread (the "nightmare" in art

is, in fact, often personified as a mare or a horse), whereas
its rhythmic manifestations betray obvious sexual tendencies.[19] In *Cumpleaños* the combination of fear and
sexual meaning connected with the apparition of horse
and rider are apparent in such phrases as "disconcerting
rhythm" and "dark steed who breathes hard with terror"
(p. 63). The sexual significance of the horseman's arrival
is further reinforced by Nuncia, who dons a gown that
gives her "a royal and pregnant look" (p. 64).

With the appearance of horse and rider the oneiric
experience seems to turn into a nightmare. A further clue
that this is so can be found in the very etymology of the
word. Jung, although concerning himself largely with its
Germanic origins, points out that it usually involves the
notion of treading (as the French *cauchemar* comes from
the Latin *calcare*, to tread), and that the experience of
having a nightmare tread upon or press upon the dreamer
has been verified by both himself and Freud in their
experience with children.[20] Thus whether Fuentes unconsciously refers to his own childhood dreams or to the
Spanish etymology of the term (*pesadilla*, probably from
pesar—to press down, to weigh—or *pisar*—to tread), the
nightmarish aspect of the work becomes fully evident
with the horseman's appearance. Evidence for this can
be found in such phrases as: "The tread of the horseman
weighed upon the gravel . . . the heavy steps of his boots
were heard in the first passage of the labyrinth. They
grew closer . . ." (p. 64). And later: "The horse neighed;
his hoofs stamped furiously against the walls; pulverized
the custodial elephants . . ." (p. 76). It is with the arrival
of horse and rider that all the anguish-producing sounds
and symbols of today's cities enter the underground fast-
ness. It is from this point, perhaps, that the novel becomes a social as well as a personal protest.

Other critics, such as George McMurray, have dealt
at length with the social preoccupations of Fuentes as

expressed in this novel. McMurray sees in *Cumpleaños*
an alienated society trapped in a precipitous race through
time and space toward its total annihilation. For him, the
novel symbolizes Fuentes's disenchantment with contemporary society and the Christian religion as well as
its normal moral values.[21]

Yet the sociological theme of protest, which may have
provided the conscious motivation for the novel, does
not in the least explain its structure. In relating this structure to the myth of Demeter and the Eleusinian initiation
rites, I do not wish to imply any conscious imitation on
the part of Fuentes. Given his cultural preoccupations,
such imitation is possible, but when dealing with such
archetypal characters as he has portrayed, conscious imitation seems the less likely possibility. These characters
are the heritage of all mythologies and all writers. It is
humanity's common experience to see the world as imperfect, as demanding sacrifice and promising rebirth.
Fuentes is not the first writer to clothe old archetypes
in new costumes, to visualize archetypal situations on
a contemporary stage. Furthermore, as we have seen, he
has been doing this since 1952.

VI
Terra Nostra, the Witch and the Apocalypse

If in the previous chapter I have dealt at some length with a novel of little more than 100 pages, the reason in part is that *Cumpleaños* is the novel most neglected by Fuentes's critics. It is too archetypal, too divorced from history, particularly Mexican history, to provide a touchstone for those critics (the majority) who always seek sociological relevancy in Fuentes's treatment of myth. (Fuentes is himself partially responsible for this since in newspaper articles, public statements, and literary essays he goes to great lengths to reassure us that his flirtations with mythology have not obscured the burning issues of our day, but have given them new importance by relating them to time-honored archetypal patterns.)

Superficially, *Cumpleaños* is not easy to relate to the Mexican experience. The world under London is a long way from Mexico City. And the two or three characters involved (counting "real" characters in Fuentes's novels has become increasingly futile since they can usually be reduced to a male and a female prototype with multiple ramifications) are too shadowy even to conform to Octavio Paz's image of the Mexican.

However, although the setting of *Cumpleaños* is not Mexico, its fatalistic thesis is more at home in Mexico than in England. The subterranean world in perpetual rotation, where the principles of destruction and creation alternate, is essentially the same as the pre-Columbian world described by Jacques Soustelle in *Daily Life of the Aztecs on the Eve of the Spanish Conquest* (trans. Patrick O'Brien [Stanford: Stanford University Press, 1970]). Of course, in *Cumpleaños* destruction and creation are individualized, personified in a single man and a single woman. Yet both are symbols. Siger, who is the narrator, is humanity. He tells us that the universe is eternal and that the eternal soul of humanity is the collective soul. The tale ends with humanity about to enter a new reincarnation, again through the vessel of life which is woman, Nuncia (whose name means *harbinger* in Spanish).

Yet *Cumpleaños* merits our interest not only because it is another example of Fuentes's Mexican fatalism. The greater importance of this little novel to our thesis is that it constitutes a rough sketch for the novel that was to occupy Fuentes for at least the next six years.

The Great Mother before *Terra Nostra*

Of course, Fuentes, like most meticulous artists, had been making sketches for *Terra Nostra* in nearly all of his previous work. Implicit or explicit in all his novels is the figure of the Great Mother, who contains both the positive and negative aspects of the anima. It is she who choreographs man's exits and entrances onto the stage of life. Whether dressed as witch, harlot, virgin, or goddess, she is also the principal actor to appear on Fuentes's novelistic stage.

Works like *Holy Place* emphasized her charismatic, masculine qualities, her real (sociological) and psychological power. In *Change of Skin* she is victim as well as witch, like Nuncia an innocent-guilty harbinger, a servant of diabolical powers which have ensnared her in the same way that she must ensnare others. In each of the works we have examined, she is viewed from the perspective of a male narrator who is obsessed by his love-hate relationship with the archetypal character. Although her words are recorded, she is always "the other." There is no novel by Fuentes where the narrator is a woman. Thus, although in his novels (especially in *Change of Skin*) he allows individual female characters to protest their stereotyped images in men's minds, after *Where the Air Is Clear*, he never permits them to break free of these stereotypes.

In short, although the female character often assumes major proportions in Fuentes's novels, she is often not really a character but a caricature of one or another aspect of the masculine unconscious. In all cases, too, the erotic episodes between the female and the male narrator are in fact symbolic reflections of the desire to capture the unconscious, to integrate it into the total personality which Jung has called "the Self." It is this quest, both psychological and metaphysical in nature, that we shall consider in our final discussion of *Terra Nostra*.

Terra Nostra and the Critics

But first let us deal with some of the structural difficulties of this novel, which one American critic describes as a "stony monument . . . which never quite comes to life in 800 pages of effort."[1] Fuentes's Mexican critics have been even less generous. An article in *El Sol* entitled "Carlos Fuentes or the Art of Fattening Books" reports that *Terra Nostra* is as large as a Sears Roebuck catalogue but not nearly so interesting. The fact is that the archetypal outlines of Fuentes's novels are by now familiar to most critics. Much of the suspense that normally propels us through a long novel is, therefore, missing. Moreover, Fuentes writes his major works with such a torrent of words and such a deluge of archetypal symbols that very few critics have the taste or the patience to navigate through to the end. There are those, however, who applaud Fuentes's ambitious scheme, if not its results. Some fellow writers, like Juan Goytisolo, have nothing but praise for Fuentes's paradigm of history. For now, clothing the archetypal skeleton of *Cumpleaños* is an ahistorical portrait of the last two thousand years in the Western world, with heroic treatment of Spain and Mexico. It is not history as Tolstoy or Stendhal would have recognized it, but archetypal history with real people, emperors and queens, compressed into single, composite figures who apparently subsume their essential characteristics. From the pen and ink sketch of *Cumpleaños*, Fuentes now mounts the scaffolding and single-handedly paints a Sistine Chapel which spans two continents.

The Preoccupation with Time

Terra Nostra is a composition preoccupied with time, both historical and mythical time (a theme we immediately recognize as a staple in Fuentes). It begins in the final year of our millennium, in the city of Paris. In mythical terms it depicts the Malthusean nightmare of uncontrolled human proliferation. Most of the following scenes are flashbacks to the Spanish court of Philip II (which included the reign of Charles V). But some episodes are set as far back as the days of Jesus, with the birth of Christianity having its dark counterpart in the graphic scenes of depravity at the Roman court of Tiberius. The final scenes bring us again to Paris almost at the moment when the twenty-first century is about to begin. Through a multitude of semihumourous schemes, the demographic explosion has given way to the impending extinction of the human race.

To trace in detail the novel's sinuosities of plot is beyond the scope of this study. However, a detailed summary appears in an article by Margaret Peden (who has excellently translated the novel into English) in the *American Hispanist* of September 1975 ("*Terra Nostra:* Fact and Fiction, pp. 4–6). Peden describes Fuentes's novel as "blasphemous, anti-clerical, anti-monarchical, scatalogical and graphic in its portrayal of sexual excesses and perversions," and at the same time "an extremely moral book," a paradox that will be discussed in the following chapter. In the meantime, let us concern ourselves with the conceptual framework of the novel.

Similarity to Earlier Novels

In spite of its revolutionary experimentalism, *Terra Nostra* has certain points in common with Fuentes's first novel. For one thing, the setting is again social, rather than completely individual. (We may recall that all his other novels are related by a single narrator and that in *Change of Skin* and *Holy Place* the narrator is a madman who sees events, both "real" and imaginary, from the confines of an asylum—the "holy place" also being an asylum in the sense of refuge from the outside world. Similarly, *Aura* and *Cumpleaños* relate the oneiric experiences of a lone and lonely narrator.)

Secondly, in *Terra Nostra*, as in *Where the Air Is Clear*, people of all social classes are represented. Fuentes's flair for popular speech is pulled out of mothballs. Finally, as in his first novel, Fuentes gives his characters broad scope for action. In this case not confined by four walls and by all the real and false memories that a narrator can crowd into them, the characters of

Terra Nostra move or swim through a world of inter-
mingling time and space with no apparent boundaries.
In conception, both novels are generous, expanding,
extroverted.

But here the similarities end. In *Terra Nostra* there
is only a limited attempt at realistic representation. The
more convincing minor characters who appear from time
to time only serve to highlight the "historical" or literary
(in the sense of being borrowed from other books) characters, who are invariably seen in archetypal terms.

And the tedium of a single narrator who drones on for
hundreds of pages is relieved by the device of multiple
narrators and multiple viewpoints. The drug-induced
hallucinations or dreams of his earlier works are replaced
by a collective dream where characters are alternately
narrators and subjects of other narrators' dreams. If
Nietzsche, Marx, and Balzac represented the ideological
skins donned by Fuentes in *Change of Skin*, in *Terra
Nostra* one senses the dream-filled, sightless eyes of
Jorge Luis Borges—a Borges who is dreaming of Cervantes, who dreams of Amadis de Gaul, who dreams of
Jesus, who is dreaming of Borges. . . .

Stylistic Devices

Terra Nostra is Fuentes's millennial novel. It is geared
to an apocryphal past, an apocalyptical future and a final
Ucronia, or timeless paradise. But the gadgetry, unlike
that in most other futuristic fiction, is taken mostly from
the present. It is gadgetry from the world of entertain-
ment, reproduction of sound and image (a natural choice
for a writer who, like his anti-hero Philip II, is enamored
of both the word and the visual image). *Terra Nostra* is
dominated by the techniques of the record player, the
tape recorder and the movies (or television)[2], gadgets

that operate within time and upon time. Yet, used in the manner of Fuentes, they generate a final vision of time-lessness, a super-Marxian synthesis that destroys the preceding dichotomies which, according to Fuentes, are the drumbeat of time.

All three, phonograph record, tape deck, and film strip, may be regarded as circles forever repeating the same tune or image, but their textures, circumferences, and objectives are not identical. Their use, sometimes si-multaneously with other devices of triplicity—the tri-partite division of the work, the triptych painting, the triplets, etc.—propels the novel (slowly) to its final hal-lucination. And time, like any large vehicle with only three wheels, is thus endowed with an inherent insta-bility that must eventually result in an accident. This at least is the hope of Fuentes, writer, producer, and di-rector, who studies the leviathan from many angles. The different facets of time, as seen by different cameramen or narrators, are revealed in a series of close-ups. Time is seen to advance at breathtaking speed; one step of the Escorial's stairway, for example, can equal a lifetime, just as Borges's second in "The Secret Miracle" could equal a year. Time can be interchangeable with space. Times "join together or are superimposed, and then sep-arate. We can travel from one time to another."[3] Fuentes's time is surrealist time, dream time. It is also "Star Trek" time, with pockets or crevices where all times meet. It is instantaneous time, which Fuentes tells us in *Tiempo Mexicano* (written during the early, conceptual stages of *Terra Nostra*) is "pure time," the urban Mexican's only answer to the crushing oppression of the past which de-nies him genuine personality.[4]

Triplicity is the magical key that opens and closes the labyrinthine structure of time. It is the explicit theme of numerous chapters in section three devoted to the teachings of the Cabala. Thus in *Terra Nostra*, which is condensed history, archetypal history, there are *three* bastards of Philip the Fair. (And here it is the fourth of the "Brothers Hapsburg," the legitimate one, who is the murderer.) Philip II in character is also an incarnation of the number three, synthesizing the positive and negative features of the student, Ludovico, and the huntsman, Guzmán. Within him they compose the triumvirate of idealism, opportunism, and power.

The Female Characters

As for the female characters of the novel, here again there are basically three: Juana la Loca (Joan the Crazy); Isabel, wife of Philip; and Celestina, the bawd, witch, go-between of Fernando de Rojas's famous novel of 1499. (The jungle sex goddess of the New World is only a variation of Celestina, since both are identified by the same tattooed lips and both are supratemporal, ageing and rejuvenating throughout the novel.) Together the three—Juana, Isabel, and Celestina—compose (like Nuncia of *Cumpleaños*) the three-faced Hecate, goddess of witchcraft (who in the New World is called "La Llorona," the witch goddess of the crossroads). The dwarf Barbarica (who seems to step straight out of the pages of José Donoso's *Obsceno pájaro de la noche* [*The Obscene Bird of Night*]), is basically an emanation of Juana, acting as her surrogate in the sexual union with the mad prince, a relationship prohibited to the old queen by her physical limitations. (To cite Fuentes's own work, she is a caricature of Aura.) Like Hecate, all three women are involved in witchcraft and in the rituals of death. Juana, who later metamorphoses into Carlota of Mexico, devotes her life to necrophilia in her mad adoration of the dead spouse. Madness, or lunacy, the mythological reference to moon goddess Hecate, marks both her historical and novelistic role. Isabel, too, becomes immersed in the cult of necrophilia, invoking diabolical powers to create her homunculus composed of bits of royal corpses.[5] Also, as befits a goddess, she contrives a sexual union with her own son, Don Juan. Finally, exercising her powers of metamorphosis, she becomes that other queen, Elizabeth of England, who avenges the past wrongs inflicted by her Spanish monarchs.

In like manner, Celestina, in revenge for her rape by Philip the Fair, reenacts the role of Nuncia and invokes the power of the Devil, thereby acquiring the relative immortality that assures her omnipresence throughout at least some four hundred chronological years of the novel. Her tattooed lips seem to be an allusion to the core of dead spiders in the famous jungle mask of feathers, and lend themselves to both Freudian and Jungian explanations. The Freudian would relate the tattooed lips to pubic hair surrounding the genital opening. (The early Neruda also equates pubic hair to spiders.) The Jungian interpretation, by far the more complex and interesting, will be discussed shortly in connection with the mask itself. For the moment let us merely observe that the three women, the two queens and Celestina (who in her New World manifestation is also a queen), in themselves and jointly combine all the positive and negative features which Jung associates with the anima figure.

The Inherent Ambiguity

Although the central character of *Terra Nostra* is apparently Philip II, Felipe, obviously the anima figure in its various forms all but dominates the novel. The wisdom

and creativity of the anima, in fact, account for the revolutionary paradise that we glimpse at the novel's end.
Yet the dominant characteristic of the archetype is ambiguity, and this *Terra Nostra* demonstrates on nearly
every one of its 778 pages (English version). The
inherent ambiguity of the work itself is sufficient to
explain the debate among critics as to whether *Terra
Nostra* was motivated by the author's hope or resigna-
tion. The Spanish novelist Juan Goytisolo tells us that
Fuentes examines the repetitive cycles of Hispanic history in order to help future generations avoid them; true
enlightenment is the best remedy against the whirlpool
of the past.[6] But Michael Wood says that Fuentes swamps
the present with memory, experiences the past as a "crip-
pling and irresistible burden, an old world which simply
eclipses all new and next worlds".[7] The paradox, pet
device of Fuentes, is that perhaps both are correct. Since
the literary space of *Terra Nostra* is open space, free for
any intelligent reader's interpretation or creation, an
inexhaustible mine for the critics, it simultaneously
swamps us with the past and extends a tenuous hope for
the future.

Thirty-three: The Importance of Numbers

Yet the dominant movement in this study of time and
history is the 33-cycle rotation of the phonograph record
that plays and replays the same tune for at least two
thousand years. There are thirty-three final days to the
Parisian apocalypse. The total cycle of the three youths'
dreams is thirty-three months. Almost identical are the
thirty-three steps through time and space and successive
incarnations in the Escorial, also the thirty-three steps
to sacrifice on the apex of the Aztec pyramid, and the

thirty-three steps in the courtyard of Montezuma's pal-
ace. There is always the implacable revolution, while
on different stages and in different disguises the same
actors play the same roles. Philip II can be detected in
various incarnations as Cortez, as Tezcatlipoca, Toltec
god of death and war, as Montezuma, as Tiberius, as
Franco, even as a wolf. Jesus appears as the three Juans,
the triplets, Quetzacoatl, and Padre Las Casas, the great
Spanish champion of the Indians. Celestina makes her
constant reappearances in the child (Celestina II?), in
La Malinche (the slave-serf, mistress of the conqueror
Cortez-Philip), and as Coatlicue, Terrible Mother of
Death, here representing the negative pole of the anima
figure.

But whereas the number three is the dynamic, positive symbol of the novel, its repetition as thirty-three
introduces ominous overtones. The pyramid, the steps
of the mausoleum, are both symbols of the death culture.
In both cases each step is an approach to extinction, a
condensation of time in the life of the individual. In his
study of Cabalistic numerology which dominates three
chapters of the third section of the novel (a coincidence?), Fuentes suggests the genesis for his repeated
"thirty-threes":

> The number eleven . . . is the arsenal of sin. It closes
> the great circle of creation and life, redemption and
> reunion. In eleven there is one small unity, a mis-
> erable one opposing divine unity: Lucifer. [In
> thirty-three even that minuscule unity is destroyed.]
> Eleven is temptation: having everything, we desire
> more. The multiples of eleven only accentuate this
> evil and misfortune: twenty-two, thirty-three . . . in-
> creasing dispersion, the always vaster separation
> between human and divine unity . . . ." (p. 529)

Technology in the Construction of *Terra Nostra*

Obviously, the 33 cycle rotation of the record interminably replaying the archetypal song of history represents a constant spinning off of unity, multiplication ad infinitum. Fuentes here insinuates both Cabalistic and Gnostic rejections of the wheel of life. And as novelist, to the monotony of the record-clock he opposes a new time based on more up-to-date technology, the tape recorder. Using the "rewind" control, he makes it possible to shoot back in time to sixteenth-century Spain, or to travel via the green bottle (a recorded message from the past) to the age of Tiberius. Author and characters utilize the same device. Felipe "rewinds" and makes possible his own succession by ancestors instead of descendants.

Fuentes grammatically renders the "fast forward" speed of the tape recorder by a breathless abandonment of punctuation and normal rules of logical sentence structure, and substantively by the final flight into the future (which also reaffirms the circular construction of the work, beginning and ending with the last day of the second millennium). "Fast forward" is also the terrible temptation of his characters, as we see when Philip makes his shattering ascent into the future via the stairway of thirty-three steps and the magic mirror that reflects this future, or when the Pilgrim in the New World faces his unremembered destiny, scenes from his own future, in the smoking mirror of Tezcatlipoca (p. 470). Most of the action in the episodes dealing with the New World rushes past in this "fast forward" speed, which is also a characteristic speed of mythology. This is perhaps one of the reasons that the section called "The New World" is for the average reader the most successful part of the novel.

The Influence of the Movies

But finally, of course, Fuentes's fascination with film accounts for the reverse effect, the numerous "holds" or "freezes" where time stands still. These are the moments of love that defy time, as Octavio Paz explained much earlier in his *Labyrinth of Solitude*. Sometimes Fuentes calls this "freeze" "woman's time," the "time that must disappear and then turn backwards until it finds the privileged moment of love and there, only there, remain forever" (p. 726). The same idea can also be found in *Aura*. And if we turn from projector to screen, we find that old Celestina functions as both, absorbing past events in her memory and then projecting them onto the white cloth that covers her face. This in turn becomes a gigantic screen, fills all the interior space of the hut that appears in the chapter entitled "Restoration" (where, significantly, the tape recorder appears substantively as a mysterious possession of the old woman).

Yet none of these devices is totally new in Fuentes. *Where the Air Is Clear* also made use of "Newsreel," "Camera Eye," and other such borrowings from Dos Passos's *Manhattan Transfer*. The major innovation here is that the projection is often stylistic rather than substantive and that its focus is Spanish history, literature, and art, plus a focus on time itself, rather than one that confines itself to the spacial limitations of a single city.

The Original Draft

Speaking in very personal terms, *Terra Nostra* was familiar to me (in specific detail as well as theme) long before it was published. In 1969 Fuentes sent me a manuscript containing most of the essential features of the chapter entitled "Restoration" (the fourth chapter from the last), as well as other sections that now appear almost verbatim throughout the course of the novel. Fuentes's intention at the time was to publish this manuscript (about the length of *Aura*) as part of an anthology of his "witches." The work was to be called *Las Viejas* (*The Old Women*). I was to write the introduction, José Luis Cuevas was to do the illustrations. When this work did not appear as scheduled, I had no idea what had happened. Fuentes was not a writer to be rejected by publishers. But with the appearance of *Terra Nostra*, I realized that Fuentes must have become enamored of this fragment and polished it, enlarged it. Again he succumbed to the spell of the anima figure, who dominates both novel and tale.

The tale is to the novel what an eerie melody played on the flute might be to a symphony full of drums and cymbals. In other words, the original is impressionistic, mysterious (dominated by Fuentes's ambivalent "tú"), basically visual and cinematographic with relatively little intellectual baggage. A detailed comparison of the two works would confirm Fuentes's remark to Emir Ròdríguez-Monegal that he is a "putter-inner and not a taker-outer."[8]

The time of the tale is again one of those moments that contain both past and future. We are told that a sand clock of Juana la Loca is running backwards (a denial of gravity and time), in addition to the detail supplied in the novel's version where it becomes a tape recorder playing backward a shattering of glass. The sixteenth-century funeral procession is juxtaposed with the Mexican band of guerilla fighters of the future, and the Juana who appears in the sand dunes seems to be a projection of the Old Woman, (amorphous here, not yet Celestina) as camera. The Old Woman, assumed to be a spy, contains and projects the characters of Carlota of Mexico and the ubiquitous jungle maiden or sorceress (who has not yet jelled into la Malinche).

In the manuscript, it is the Old Woman who manifests the overwhelming fear of fragmentation, multiplicity. "Two bodies because they are apart are immediate enemies. One life is inadequate to reconcile two different bodies," she says to her captor.[9] And so in more than the purely sexual sense she attempts to become one with a reincarnated lover. Their synchronized breathing is a frustrated attempt at real fusion. (In the novel this scene is inexplicably reduced to the statement: "the old woman imitates the breathing of the wounded man . . ." [p. 728]. Life itself, as incarnate in this anima figure, is here the protagonist in the search for unity and the cessation of time. Fuentes elaborates the same idea most completely in the final chapter of the novel, but in the fragment I find it more poetic and aesthetically satisfying in that it fails. The Old Woman is shot (though the jungle maiden puts in a final appearance).

The Mask/Map

In both works, however, the symbol of the mask/map of feathers is of paramount importance. Like so much of *Terra Nostra*, it is open to a variety of interpretations. In his article, "El Mapa y la Máscara," Pedro Gimferrer limits himself basically to only one of them, a fairly provincial one that equates both mask and map to a terrifying face which denies us our individual identities, substituting for them the history of the Hispanic world.[10] This may well be the conscious meaning that Fuentes himself gives to the symbol. But in this interpretation the idea of map is subordinated to the idea of mask perceived as subterfuge, disguise. From a modern viewpoint, mask and map are diametrically opposed: the former is to conceal, the latter to reveal. Yet regarded rather from the viewpoint of antiquity, both objects serve as representations of an intangible reality, the individual persona or the world.

Fuentes attributes the inspiration for his map/mask of feathers at various points to Roberto Matta, owner of the map (see the acknowledgements, *Terra Nostra*), and also to Fernando Benítez's *Los indios de México*,[11] where the mask functions as part of the religious ceremonies of the Cora Indians (described on pages 718–19 in *Terra Nostra*). Yet also, as in Dante, the mask serves as a guide to the universe so that the lovers may once again find each other. In *Terra Nostra*, the mysterious object is constantly being woven or spun by the Indian maiden (whose tattooed lips suggest the spinning spiders), or by the Old Woman with the huge white face, Celestina, Hecate, moon goddess. As Mircea Eliade tells us: "It is the Moon that spins time; it is the Moon that spins human existences . . . the goddesses of destiny are spinners."[12] Therefore, the feathered object may be considered a map of destiny, a clock of transcendental time. The weaving and reweaving of the Old Woman is like the winding of life's clock. The arrow-tipped feathers, symbols which represent spirit as opposed to matter, suggest the vain attempt by man to escape the limits of time and space, the hope that is ever frustrated by the magnetic center of spiders which is the forbidden part of the jungle, where "dwell the masters of words, signs and enchantments" (p. 717). Among other things, the map/mask can also represent the space-time continuum. The perfect circularity of the center again emphasizes the implacable wheel of life.[13]

Yet in *Terra Nostra* the spinning of time eventually does come to a stop, on the last page of the novel. The circular sweep of history succumbs to the dialectic of change, of history moving in an ascending spiral. Its apex, as seen by Fuentes, is far beyond the classless society envisioned by Marx. Fuentes's is a biological radicalism, quite in tune with modern feminism of the far left. Only with androgyny, he says, is the ultimate dichotomy, that of male-female, resolved and the tolling of history stopped. This, as I see it, is why the clock of the last sentence fails to strike and the pale sun of Paris emerges after the cessation of snow. (The Mexican sun, like many Latin American writers, seems to have migrated to the cultural oasis in the more northerly latitude of Paris.)

The Aztec Heritage

But the sun symbol reminds us again of the Aztec component in Fuentes's obsession with time. Within the novel, Fuentes's cultural heritage is most pronounced in section two, where the narrator's fate is determined by his ability to intuit sacred time, the time created by the gods that can be stretched out or condensed according to divine whim. Here the narrative suggests the form and content of the Mayan Popol Vuh with generous infusions from Fray Bernadino de Sahagún (and his tale of the historic Toltec ruler, Quetzalcoatl, which appears in the General History of the Things of New Spain (ed. A. M. Garibay, 4 vols. [Mexico, P. F.: Editorial Porrúa, 1956], Bernal Díaz del Castillo, Cortez, and the Aztec poetic laments from Miguel Leon-Portilla's *Visión de los Vencidos (The Broken Spears)*. Myth and history are blended with such skill in this section that the seams are almost imperceptible. Only here does Fuentes manage to succeed in the very task in which his character, Isabel, La Señora, fails. He creates a homunculus, a live body of narrative out of fragments of the dead past. Per-

haps his success is due to the simpler narrative technique, in addition to the faster pace already mentioned,
that distinguishes this section from the rest of the novel.
The reader can focus on the character of a single narrator
without dissipating his attention and intellectual energy
in a guessing game with the author. And although the
Cortez (alias "Pilgrim") of this section is a composite of
the fictional Guzmán, Tezcatlipoca, Quetzalcoatl (both
historical and mythological versions), and of Philip II
himself, the splitting is pyschological, not physical. Fiction here reinforces modern pyschology, representing
the schizophrenic personality in all its mythological trap-
pings. The persona, Quetzalcoatl or Las Casas, is only
the sunlit part of the personality whose shadow (the subconscious double), is represented by Tezcatlipoca or
Guzmán.

Perhaps the success of this section may also be explained by Fuentes's profound assimilation of his Mexican heritage. He acquired the historical data on the
reign of Philip II, the Jewish community of Toledo, the
Cabala, etc. by research in libraries and through con-
sultations with scholars, as his acknowledgments clearly
show. This information was consciously absorbed and
committed to paper. But it was not given time to ferment
deep within the writer's unconscious, as had Mexican
mythology and history. Since 1954 in his *Los días enmascarados,* Fuentes has been obsessed with Mayan
rain gods and with "what Octavio calls 'the enchantress,
the witch, the white serpent.' "[14] The mirror of Philip,
for example, seems to be a spin-off of the real mirror, the
smoking mirror of Tezcatlipoca, which is the key to the
future.[15] And the leaps in time that Fuentes arranges
with such artifice in the first and last, or predominantly
European, sections of the work are remarkably natural
in the mythological setting of ancient Mexico, with its
sacred time and its masked days outside of time. The

tryst with a reincarnated enchantress which seems forced in a European setting succeeds in the ambiance of a mythological past. Like the African explorer in H. Rider Haggard's *She*, Fuentes's pilgrim can convincingly dream of a future reunion with the old-young enchantress in some subsequent incarnation of them both. This is the archetypal dream that Fuentes has been committing to paper since "Tlactocatzine" of *Los días enmascarados*, but nowhere does it glow with such technicolor as in *Terra Nostra*.

Yet the dark Mexican fatalism, forged in the ancient cosmogeny of self-destroying worlds, is also sharply evident in this section. The Aztec suns, nourished only by human sacrifice, are never far below the horizon of Fuentes's thoughts. *Tiempo Mexicano*, Fuentes's collection of essays published in 1972, is predicated upon the existence of a fatalistic past which permeates the psychology of the modern Mexican intellectual, a "Narcissus condemned to stare at himself in the bottom of a cup of instant coffee; a Prometheus chained to his psychiatrist's couch."[16] According to Fuentes, indigenous stereotypes metamorphose into modern slogans; revolution is a restoration of the original past[17] (an idea that Octavio Paz had developed in *Postdata*, published in 1970). The old gods, Huichilobos and Coatlicue, gods of war and death, continue to have their devoted following. Even Quetzalcoatl, the only god who dared to appear in human form—the protagonist of both creation and the fall—sowed in the Mexican soul an infinite conviction of circularity.[18]

Yet paradoxically Fuentes finds an escape, or perhaps only a desire for escape, from the infinite circle in the very Mexican art that depicts the monolithic figure of Coatlicue ("purveyor of red hearts in winter"). She, unlike the humanoid Quetzalcoatl, is portrayed as headless, stable, immobile, a guarantee against the apocalypse, the negation of a future which could only lead to catastrophe. And when future is suppressed, says Fuentes, men's imaginations revert to the distant past, to their origins, to longing for a prehistoric state of original unity.[19] He senses that the anonymous creators of these incarnations of immobility projected their human desires and imaginations into the stone: "In the land of necessity desires become transfigured in order to reach their forbidden objective."[20]

Fuentes therefore considers pre-Columbian art to be modern art, a form of surrealism. This he defines as "a revolt against the order of things, a desperate and spectacular exercise of memory and imagination in order to rediscover the forgotten—the sources of the beginning and of unity."[21]

The Third Millennium and the Apocalypse

Fuentes, like his fellow Mexican artists of the surreal, is forever going back to the beginnings, to Genesis. So the critic, too, may perhaps hazard the observation that the genesis of *Terra Nostra* is surely the approaching of the third millennium and the apocalyptic forebodings that this inspires in the Aztec psyche of its author. Are we witnessing the final days of the fifth sun, and perhaps the prelude to another painful re-creation? In building the intricate leviathan of *Terra Nostra* has not Fuentes also been seeking the same aperture in the circle of destiny sought by his ancestors and revealed to him by contemplation of their immobile stone gods? Yet the tools available to Fuentes are infinitely more subtle, and of enviable variety.

Fuentes reaches out to all the giants of Spanish and Latin American literature, and also to Dante, Dostoevski, Saint Thomas More, Hegel, Marx, Americo Castro, and

Paz, of course—to mention only some of the most important and obvious coauthors of *Terra Nostra*. And as he indicates in *Tiempo Mexicano,* Fuentes also relies partly on the ideas of the Spanish philosopher Eugenio Imaz, in his *Topía y Utopía.* According to Imaz, Utopia was a misleading concept. Although this idea of paradise, or the unity of mankind, was historically inspired by the discovery of the New World, it should never have been couched in spatial terms or even in aspatial terms. Certainly More knew it could not exist on earth. Only after the development of nineteenth-century dialectical thought—a temporal mechanism—was it possible to imagine a Utopia existing in a future No Time, rather than a No Place. Utopia could only be Ucronia. And for time to cease, the dialectic of history—all the Manichaean dichotomies—would have to come to an end.[22]

The ultimate fusion of male-female that this thinking produces in the last pages of the novel is almost a caricature of Jung's idea of the integration of the personality.[23] Jung had said that man must come to terms with his unconscious self, the shadow or double and especially the anima, in order not to project them onto others as love or hate objects, in order to find personal and social peace. But of course this would be an integration of the mind, not of the body. Fuentes's vision, undoubtedly influenced by the philosophy of body presented by Octavio Paz in his *Conjunciones y disyunciones,* is not androgynous (in the manner of angels, that is, sexless) so much as hermaphroditic, with the possibility of an infinite number of erotic combinations. It is almost a pornographic version of Jung, the same tune, but this time played not on the harp but on the saxophone; the same tune we've heard before but orchestrated, syncopated, intensified in volume and designed to tumble down the walls of the third millennium.

VII
Terra Nostra and the Androgyne

Fuentes has called himself a "pornographic novelist" or at least a writer of "pornographic passages."[1] Yet in the case of *Terra Nostra*, one would have to be a most determined lover of pornography to plough through eight hundred pages of history, religion, philosophy, etc. in order to find its few pornographic episodes. Some, such as the orgy in Tiberius's court, blend unobtrusively into the setting of Roman corruption. But the final and most pornographic passage, the self-copulation of the male-female narrator, creates a disturbing conclusion for a novel that is largely metaphysical.

Of course we understand that Fuentes had somehow to finish *Terra Nostra*. With his usual flair for the dramatic, he reserves the major shock treatment for the end. Out of the sexual acrobatics of the last surviving character will emerge a new race of people living in perpetual harmony. Out of pornography he promises paradise. The old world ends in super-orgasm. Such an explanation for the conclusion of *Terra Nostra* is temptingly simple, but it does not take into account that Fuentes's latest novel is also the climax of his longstanding flirtation with the idea of androgyny.

The Androgynous Ideal

Beginning with *Holy Place*, one could trace the development of the androgynous ideal which Fuentes sees as a solution to most of his major preoccupations—those of time, death, social alienation, and the implacable cycle of history. However, the major drawback to the androgynous solution as presented on the final pages of *Terra Nostra* is that these existential problems relate to the psyche and the sphere of religion, whereas the resolution is blatantly sexual. Perhaps the shock is deliberate and the explanation lies in the words of one of Fuentes's characters from *Cantar de ciegos*, an artist defending his conversion to pop art: "Before I tried to say that a sacred art is possible among us. . . . That wasn't true. . . . Neither the earth nor man is sacred today. This is what is sacred. This ultimate bit of profanity. What I offer them. The negation of all that is sacred. What they use."[2]

In short, this may be what we, as middle class consumers of pornography, deserve. And perhaps Fuentes, like Aristophanes who is made by Plato to discuss the androgyne in startlingly biological terms,[3] is playing the comedian. But whatever the reason (and we shall return to it by way of conclusion), the incongruity between problem and solution accounts for the disconcerting effect of *Terra Nostra's* final pages. They demonstrate the danger—cited by Carolyn Heilbrun and many others —of confusing androgyny, an ideal, with hermaphroditism, an anomalous physical condition.[4]

For Heilbrun the androgynous novel is one in which readers of both sexes can identify with the hero.[5] True heroines for her are heroes in that they combine the positive qualities normally considered masculine with the sensitivity associated with the feminine. But obviously this criterion cannot be applied to *Terra Nostra*, where reader identification with characters who have no fixed identities of their own is completely out of the question.

We must rather examine on the level of pure myth and symbol whether *Terra Nostra* is an androgynous novel. By reference to Cirlot's *Diccionario de símbolos*, we find that androgyny represents an integrated dualism in the human being. Cirlot points out that all peoples have considered their first gods androgynous, and the origins of their race as mental rather than physical. Yet he also tells us that before expressing this idea in metaphysical terms, magical religious thought has often made use of a biological frame of reference.[6]

The Androgyne and the Hermaphrodite

For Mircea Eliade, however, the dichotomy between biological and spiritual androgyny is fundamental. He contrasts the angelic Séraphita, a sexless being, of Balzac[7] to the hermaphrodite of satanic or morbid literature which for him represents the degradation of the androgyne as a symbol. This symbol he traces back to the Platonic myth about the original round beings whose impertinence resulted in the divine punishment of being cut into two parts, each half eternally seeking the other.[8] Even the Platonic story is apparently only one example of a universal myth of a golden age, which psychologically refers to the paradisiacal state of unity which man seeks magically to recapture.

The return to this original unity has been symbolized ritually in the initiation rites and wedding ceremonies that Eliade describes and especially in Carnival, or the fiesta whose metaphysical implications have also been noted by both Octavio Paz and Fuentes.[9] As Eliade explains, carnivals and orgies represent a symbolic restoration of the undifferentiated unity or chaos that pre-

ceded the creation of the world. Mythically and
psychologically they effect a new immersion in the lim-
itless power existing before creation, and they take place
in order to assure the success of a new beginning.[10] But
Eliade draws a sharp distinction between ritual orgy on
the one hand and the realization of totality that can be
achieved by meditation and other Yogic techniques. The
first is a desperate effort that replaces these complex and
esoteric techniques by concrete, physiological means.[11]

Earlier Hermaphrodites in Fuentes's Work

Fuentes's works provide a number of examples of this
ritualistic or orgiastic androgynization discussed by
Eliade. Like Siberian shamans, for example, "Mito" of
Holy Place tries to become part of the hermaphroditic
Claudia through fetishism.[12] His twin, Giancarlo, resorts
to orgy and the ritual of simulated birth in order to integrate with the female.[13] In *Change of Skin* Herr Urs
creates hermaphroditic dolls and paintings of chaotic
horror [14] in what we now realize is a technique for simulating Carnival and its inherent powers, while the narrator of the same novel makes use of a final orgy in order
to re-create his disintegrating personality. The fact that
he calls the emanations of his imagination "monks"
underlines their religious significance. Except in *Terra
Nostra,* all these frantic, confused attempts to achieve
by shortcut what has always been the most transcendent
goal of mankind fail. In this sense they are realistic
novels.

The Archetype of the Circle

Yet on a certain level, ritual androgynization can be successful. This may be explained by reference to the Jung-

ian concept of the two circles. In the previous chapter, I have discussed the archetype of the circle in Fuentes mainly as a symbol of rebirth and continuity. Yet like all archetypes, it is susceptible to many interpretations. Jung considers the circle to be the most fundamental archetype of all found at the deepest level of the collective unconscious. Just as the anima appears only after the shadow, and the personal unconscious, have been exorcised, so the full meaning of the circle becomes apparent only after the other inhabitants of the collective unconscious have been recognized and at least partially assimilated to consciousness. On the level of anima, the circle appears as a life symbol, a womb symbol. But when we encounter it on its deepest level, it is a symbol of God, original wholeness or "self" as Jung called it, "the totality of the psyche."[15]

One of the basic problems for religion and psychology is the proliferation of levels on which the self symbol can occur, since the self is not only the centre, but also the whole circumference which embraces conscious and unconscious."[16] Although Jung first thought that we could experience self only when we reach middle age, Edward Edinger has postulated the experience by young children and primitive peoples of the uroborus or tail-eater, a kind of primordial self.[17] Drawings by very young children, for example, portray the human being as a circle. But this circle is a self that has not separated from the ego.[18] It is apparently this self that can be recaptured through orgy and all those celebrations suggestive of return to the womb. However, after the adult has learned to separate ego from unconscious, there is a growing awareness of a universal self of which the unconscious self was only the tiniest part, the microcosm of the macrocosm. In Gnosticism, to which Fuentes refers again and again in fiction and in his numerous essays (especially in *Cervantes o la crítica de la lectura* [Mexico, D.F.: Joaquín Mortiz, 1976], this universal self is

equated with God. In Jungian psychology it is expressed
as the "integration of the personality."

The Mandala

This metaphysical process is often represented in religion and psychology by the mandala, the archetype of
wholeness. The mandala is literally that which encloses
graphically a circle. Frequently there are several circles
and also a square or other quaternary symbol, all having
the same central point. The quaternary symbol represents the individual and personal, or the ego, and the
outer circle the highest unity or quintessence.[19]
    In other words, the true androgyne is a symbol of unity
or wholeness, and if it exists in Fuentes's works, it must
be found not in hermaphroditic representation but in the
arcane language of geometric symbols. Jung considers
the square, the cross and crucifixion, the house, the
church, and the city as quaternary symbols, part of the
mandala. Fuentes, however, favors a preponderance of
ternary symbols in *Terra Nostra*—triptychs, triplets, etc.
He quotes the Cabala: "three is the creative number,
and without it form and matter would be inert" (p. 529).

Quaternary and Ternary Symbols in *Terra Nostra*

The differing numerical emphasis in Fuentes and Jung
in fact reflects a conflict among psychologists concerning
the primacy of the archetypes three and four. For Jung,
three was a defective quaternity[20] whereas others like
Fuentes have been impressed with the importance of
three in Gnosticism, the Cabala and Egyptian and other
mythologies. Edward Edinger, a Jungian psychologist,

tries to solve the dilemma by considering three the archetype of dynamism of the life process, whereas four
is the static symbol of the perfect self never to be ob-
tained. In short, three symbolizes process, four symbolizes goal.[21] If there is greater emphasis on three than on
four in *Terra Nostra* it is because the novel is essentially
a study of the historical process unfolding in time. Yet
the final chapter is called "The Last City," a quaternary
image, and must be taken as part of the first chapter,
"Flesh, Sphere, Gray Eyes beside the Seine," which is
charged with allusions to the circle.

The entire narrative starts at four o'clock in the morning of 14 July. The quaternary image of the Eiffel Tower
is counterpoised to the circular flight of a vulture. The
character of Pollo Phoibee, the original protagonist, is
presented within the double square of his billboards,
whereas a double circle of penitents forms before the
church of Saint Germain. From the center of the double
circle, a monk anathematizes those heretics who believe
in a spherical reincarnation. The quaternary impact is
further enhanced by the inclusion of the four cardinal
points in the description of the boundaries of the larger
circle of penitents. And finally there is the reference to
Celestina's chalk drawing on the asphalt bridge: "from
a black circle radiated colored triangles, blue, garnet,
green and yellow; Pollo tried to remember where he had
only recently seen a similar design" (p. 27). What can
this design be but a mandala divided into a quaternity
of four colors, the very same colors whose radiating design is to be repeated in the equally symbolic mask of
feathers? We may now realize that in the final chapter,
"The Last City," the donning of the mask serves as prelude to the realization of unity, graphically portrayed in
the biological creation of the hermaphrodite.

Clearly, therefore, the mandala is a significant symbol
in Fuentes's iconography. As in Tibetan Buddhism, it

seems to serve as a ritual instrument or Yantra to assist in meditation concerning its ultimate goal.[22] Yet it need not be a conscious device on Fuentes's part. Jung tells us that it occurs spontaneously in drawings by patients struggling with the problem of opposites in human nature.[23] In its quaternary component it has also been commented upon by Befumo Boschi and Elisa Calabrese, who discuss the importance of the cross in several of Fuentes's earlier works (i.e., *Aura, Holy Place, Artemio Cruz,* and *Change of Skin*) and who consider it, just as Jung does, a mediator between the conscious and the unconscious personality.[24] Also of significance for Fuentes, according to Boschi and Calabrese, is the archetype of the number six, which in the Cabala is the number of creation. This can be demonstrated in *Terra Nostra* by the frenzy of reproduction described in the opening chapter, where all the cross-marked infants have six toes. Throughout *Terra Nostra* as in Platonic philosophy and in the Cabala, "we see numbers serving as intermediaries between ideas—between the supreme concept and the objects which are its incomplete manifestation in the world."[25]

Finally, in both opening and closing chapters we find the important quaternity of the open window which Pollo sees as "the visible symbol of liberty" (p. 11). When he closes the window in the first chapter, he feels that the world is irremediably growing older. The entire narration with its reincarnated ghosts takes place only after Pollo closes the window, draws the heavy drapes and creates a magic, sunless world of destiny similar to the subterranean city of *Cumpleaños*. Without the aperture or quaternity of the window, we are engulfed in the dark world of the unconscious. But in the last line of the novel, once the window has been opened again, the image of the mandala reappears, the sphere of cold sun within the organized quaternity of the window frame. Now even the adjective "cold" may have multiple significance. With the fusion of opposites initiated by the hermaphroditic creation, the "cold" sun could well symbolize the Tantric fusion of sun and moon, the masculine and feminine principles of nature. Thus in the new Genesis, of which androgynization is only one aspect, according to Mircea Eliade, we should also expect the abolition of all the other Manichaean dichotomies beginning with day-night, light-darkness.[26]

These few examples from two chapters of *Terra Nostra* are chosen merely to show that on the metaphysical level the work has many features which we might call androgynous in their reference to the principle of original and ultimate wholeness. At the conclusion of chapter one there is also the specific comparison between the fall of Pollo and that of Icarus, the fall being a conspicuous element in the myth of androgyny. In the Jungian interpretation Icarus, in turn, is compared to Plato's original round beings. His inflated personality, like theirs, is punished by a fall or disintegration.[27] Such an explanation would also serve as the rationale for the multiple narrators who split off from Pollo after his fall into the river, and attain wholeness again only at the androgynous conclusion.

The question now arises whether all these archetypes and symbols are the product of Fuentes's collective unconscious, or deliberate intellectual allusions. The truth, I believe, lies somewhere between both hypotheses. Although he may not have read Jung directly, Fuentes is obviously familiar with most of his ideas and even his terminology. Twice in the final chapter he says, "Several lifetimes are needed to integrate a personality" (pp. 769, 774), using typically Jungian terms. In his recent interview with Marcelo Coddou, in fact, Fuentes specifically refers to the mandala as the spacial and temporal symbol expressing his aspiration to simultaneity in the construction of *Terra Nostra*.[28]

In short, I believe that Fuentes is well aware of the incongruity of resolving a spiritual dilemma of the highest order on the lower level of the hermaphrodite. In its revival of the primitive Egyptian myth of a self-copulating world creator, *Terra Nostra* is clearly at odds with the Western, sophisticated nature of metaphysical thought and even with the original Egyptian myth which Jung explains as symbolic of a nourishing of present life and not as new procreation.[29] Though Fuentes argues that *El libro de buen amor* (*The Book of Good Love*, by the Archpriest of Hita) is a practical example of how "eroticism and religion can and must coexist,"[30] the synthesis to which he alludes, as we have seen, can take place only on the level of primary unconsciousness, the level of ritual. This was the level of androgynous yearning realized through the sexual act in *Aura*,[31] *Cumpleaños*, and *Change of Skin*. And although the distinction is not critical to my argument, in all these earlier novels we were dealing with more or less genuine eroticism, (not admitted pornography), a genuine eroticism such as that found in the Song of Solomon, which may be taken metaphorically.[32]

The Importance of the Body in *Terra Nostra*

All of this leaves us with the original question of why Fuentes saw fit to portray the consummation of androgyny in graphically sexual terms. The answer, in part, may be implicit in the problem. For example, Jung himself often shows within the mandala a schematic portrayal of a human figure. We seem to have an inherent tendency to see the self, even in psychic terms, clothed in human anatomy. The Zohar also represents the ten Sephiroth, or prime elements of the world, in the form of ten concentric circles *or* as the human body.[33] And in the particular case of Fuentes the source of inspiration, as well as the expression of it, seems to be frequently related to the visual arts. We are told by Emir Rodríguez-Monegal that it was Alberto Gironella's parodic painting of the Spanish Hapsburg court, a caricature of Velásquez, that helped generate the historic setting for *Terra Nostra*.[34]

Another painting, the version by José Luis Cuevas of Van Eyck's "Marriage of the Arnolfini," may also have inspired the more metaphysical aspect of the novel. In his discussion of this work, Fuentes foreshadows his approach to *Terra Nostra* by observing: "Times and spaces of characters and spectators penetrate each other; so do identities."[35] This interaction between painting and viewer becomes a prominent motif in *Terra Nostra*, where the painting from Orvieto almost takes on the role of a character (much like the photo in Julio Cortázar's "Las Babas del Diablo"), shaping the action and in turn being shaped by it.

Fuentes's Visual Approach to Literature

Perhaps these few examples are enough to demonstrate Fuentes's highly visual approach to literature. Whether it be via the movie screen or the canvass, ideas are generated by visual impressions, despite the fact that Fuentes is constantly struggling against the domination of the purely visual. In his short story "Fortuna lo que Ha Querido," he has a Cuevas-like hero say:

We've been using our eyes for painting ever since six centuries ago. Everything is optics. Do you re-

alize what a limitation that is?. . . As if we did not
have other organs. Everyone tries to use his
eyes. . . . And Oedipus only understood when he
became blind . . . with your eyes open, you don't
understand anything.[36]

Throughout Fuentes's work we find a conflict between
the visual, daylit impression, and the deeper knowledge
imparted by the subconscious in the world of darkness.
We may remember that in *Where the Air Is Clear* Robles
finds his true self only in the darkened room of the blind
Hortensia Chacon. The world of psychic reality portrayed in *Cumpleaños* is also a dark, subterranean one.
Yet a highly detailed and graphic representation of the
insights imparted by the dark muse cannot be resisted
by Fuentes—all of which makes for surrealist literature.

And finally there is the well-documented influence of
the movies in nearly all of Fuentes's works, the movies
as inspiration and the movie-going public with its pornographic tastes as a possible mass consumer of the literary work. In the case of *Terra Nostra* and its more than
six-year period of gestation, at least one ·of the foetal
stages resembles a movie script of the novel. Dedicated
to Luis Buñuel and entitled *Nowhere*,[37] it is part of an
anthology consisting largely of previously published
works by Fuentes. This book, called *Cuerpos y ofrendas*
(*Bodies and Offerings*), which appeared in 1972, contains an introduction by Octavio Paz that illuminates the
common obsession of both writers with the cult of the
body. Paz writes: "The body occupies a central position
in Fuentes' universe. And the revelation it provides is
suprahuman, whether it be animal or divine. It wrenches
us out of ourselves and casts us into another life, to another death, a fuller one."[38] Paz's very choice of words
is significant. For any Jungian, the reference to a reve-

lation that is both animal and divine clearly points to the
archetype of the self.

The Metaphysical Rationale

In conclusion, therefore, we may say that Fuentes, because he is Fuentes, a revolutionary, sensual writer with
a love-hate relationship to the visual and the purely intellectual, returns to the archaic myth of the hermaphrodite in order to express a metaphysical truth. He does
this consciously, aware of the discrepancy between sig-
nified and signifier. But if he uses a shortcut to a highly
esoteric goal, it is perhaps because of a feeling of urgency
that is not confined to Fuentes. Today not only novelists,
but also men of science, are warning us that our aggressive instincts may catapult us into extinction far sooner
than we think. Spain's famous neurosurgeon, Dr. José
Delgado, for example, has stated that unless we curb
human aggression before the year 2000, we may never
live to see the twenty-first century.[39] Some of the meth-
ods that Delgado has employed to curb aggression, such
as the surgical implantation of electrodes in the brain,
may be just as shocking to our aesthetic and ethical tastes
as Fuentes's vision of hermaphroditic intercourse.

In proposing an androgynous solution to aggressive
masculinity, Fuentes, in fact, is very close to the viewpoint of Heilbrun who points out that Shakespeare also,
in such plays as *The Winter's Tale* and *King Lear*, "imag-
ined a world which, because it is androgynous in its
spiritual impulses, is redeemable . . . ."[40] Even the an-
atomical hermaphrodite, which Mircea Eliade tells us
was considered an aberration of nature and destroyed in
the ancient world, [41] may be less repugnant than a twentieth-century human monster controlled by electrodes.

In other words, it is not enough for the enlightened few to contemplate their mandalas and experience an integration of the personality. Like Dostoevski's "Grand Inquisitor" Fuentes is trying to bring the vision down to the level of the mass market, to save everyone or no one. Perhaps this is the final explanation for the shock treatment on the last pages of *Terra Nostra*.

VIII
The Hydra Head and the Tale

If *Terra Nostra* was one climax of Fuentes's novelistic production, *The Hydra Head* (New York: Farrar, Straus and Giroux, 1978) marks a kind of interlude in which Fuentes may hopefully recover some of the average readers who gave up on his mythological tours de force. For here, despite the mythological title, the most conspicuous myth is that of James Bond.

Discussing the book with me before its publication, Fuentes described it as a spy mystery thriller about a poor, third-world James Bond who has none of the gadgets available to his more affluent counterparts who work for the superpowers. Fuentes made it sound like a book he did not take too seriously, and the few critical reviews it has already received tend to agree. Anthony Burgess declares: "Perhaps the true distinction of the novel resides in its having forever dispensed with the possibilities of the spy thriller as a serious form."[1]

Obviously *The Hydra Head* was not only inspired by the movies (it is dedicated to the memory of Conrad Veidt, Sydney Greenstreet, Peter Lorre, and Claude Rains, in strict order of disappearance), but was probably written for the movies. It is unlikely to elicit the kind of detailed critical attention that most of his preceding fictional works have inspired. In it Fuentes appears to be treading water, keeping his two bent forefingers in shape pounding the typewriter keys until he can take off in some new and revolutionary direction. Perhaps, like *Cumpleaños*, it is the first draft of a new super-novel. The fact is that Fuentes never wastes an idea. Even if it is a lemon, he squeezes it for all the juice it is capable of producing—in novels, plays, or journalistic writing. In this, at least, he is very puritanical.

For the critic, therefore, the real mystery behind *The Hydra Head* is this: is it the end of a particular trail that Fuentes has pursued since the beginning of his career, or is it the key to a new Carlos Fuentes?

Despite his intentional parody of Ian Fleming, here Fuentes has produced a novel that is far from a carbon copy of its English counterparts. It is a hybrid creation, unmistakably Fuentes's in its ambivalence with respect to Nietzsche and Marx, free will and fate. Yet here, in contrast to *Change of Skin*, we cannot identify Fuentes with any single character. Not only is the protagonist devoid of gadgets, but he usually appears also devoid of understanding and even of basic intelligence. He is the hapless tool of the powers that be, carries out orders he does not understand, and winds up losing even his own name, face, and personality. In short, rather than James Bond, he seems like a replay of Felipe Montero of *Aura*.

A Heroine of Three Parts

As we may now also begin to suspect, Félix Maldonado is not the only familiar character. Although there are no recognizable witches, his female counterpart is split into three women: the femme fatale, Mary; the Sophia figure of intelligence and inspiration, Sara; and the Great Mother who includes the other two, his wife Ruth. Characteristically wise, Ruth understands her role in Félix's

life. She explains to him, "I'm both of them but only half
of each" (p. 38);[2] "What I wanted to give you in me,
united in me, you'd rather have from two women. It's
as if you wanted to go back, to be young again." (p. 39).
In Jungian terms we might say that the anima, incarnate
here in the Great Mother, interprets the protagonist's
splitting her up as a denial of normal maturation, as
symptomatic of an unconscious desire by Félix to go
back to the womb. In Ruth, Fuentes creates a promising
character who might have easily developed along the
lines of Elizabeth in *Change of Skin*. But Félix, who
refers to her as a Jewish mother, implicitly recognizing
her maternal role, cannot accept her diagnosis. So he
walks out on her and her unwanted advice for nearly the
entire duration of the novel. Only at the end does she
reappear, finally revealed as the archenemy, the elusive
nun whom Félix has long suspected as an accomplice
in the murder of Sara Klein. Yet whether Ruth becomes
the Terrible Mother because of jealousy and Félix's rejection or for political revenge (Sara having defected to
the Arab cause) is never completely clear. In any case,
her costume of a nun may well suggest the anima's protean powers of transformation. From Earth Mother she
becomes the *vagina dentata*.

Sex and danger are similarly entertwined in Mary, who
with her violet eyes and sparkling bosom is variously
described as resembling Joan Bennett or Hedy Lamarr.
Yet all we learn about Mary—other than the tantalizing
details of her physical anatomy—is that she was cheer-
fully deflowered by Félix on Central Park West, and,
that in spite of a financially successful marriage and children, she continues to enjoy an intimate relationship
with the hero. What makes Mary tick, other than her
generous endowment of libido, is just another one of
those mysteries that are not cleared up in this novel.

Finally, the pivot of all the action from our hero's viewpoint is Sara, child of the Holocaust and the ideal woman of Félix's life. Of the three, Sara is the only woman who is granted a genuine and heroic history. Honest, courageous, self-sacrificing, beautiful, brainy, she is the most idealized woman to appear in any of Fuentes's novels. It is almost as if the strain of supporting her on so high a pedestal were more than the author could bear. So Sara is conveniently murdered—fairly early in the narrative— and for the passionate Félix the question of who killed Sara becomes more significant than the chase for top secret information which pits him against an assortment of Arab and Israeli spies.

Appraisal of the Novel as Spy Thriller

The main trouble with Sara was that she was literally too good to be true. And the main trouble with *The Hydra Head* is that it also fails to convince us on a number of scores. Since it is said to be a spy thriller, it must first be judged according to the standards of this genre. True, there is plenty of action. Chapter endings are carefully plotted to rush the reader straight through the book. Yet the mainspring of action never seems to lie inside the characters, but outside the narrative in the nimble fingers of Fuentes. The highly volatile Félix, whose fist sees a lot more action than his brain, is too easily convinced to become a spy and subsequently walks through his adventures almost like a somnambulist. Surely even third-world intelligence could come up with someone better qualified than Félix.

Apart from credibility of character, *The Hydra Head* can also be faulted in the matter of questionable details. It may be exotic for the Mexican reader to see his two spies communicating with each other via cryptography based on the works of Shakespeare and Lewis Carroll (all of which must be translated into Spanish footnotes in the original version), yet Sor Juana Inés de la Cruz or even Cervantes would have been a more natural choice, assuming that Fuentes was determined to provide a literary key. There are other details that sound as if they had been lifted from the latest James Bond movie. The technology encapsulated in the stone of Professor Bernstein's ring, which through laser beams reveals the entire geologic picture of Mexico's mineral deposits, has the sound of science fiction gadgetry rather than present-day possibilities.

Fuentes as Journalist

On the positive side, of course, the matter of Mexican oil reserves is certainly grist for the mill of spy thrillers. In choosing this headline topic long before the Iranian situation catapulted it into prominence, Fuentes shows the instincts of an excellent journalist. Yet unfortunately for Fuentes, Mexican President Lopez Portillo sabotaged much of the *raison d'être* of the international espionage rivalry by publicly revealing figures on his nation's probable and proven reserves. Nevertheless, we can hardly blame Fuentes for Lopez Portillo's pulling the rug out from under a sizeable chunk of plot. It is the risk anyone takes in dealing with current politics and not history, and politics continues to be one of Fuentes's passionate interests.

But it is precisely here that the novel is most open to serious attack. Although *The Hydra Head* provides a natural vehicle for Fuentes's logical, legalistic mind, as in *Change of Skin*, Fuentes becomes carried away by his own role of devil's advocate. That, at least, would be the more generous interpretation of the novel, an interpretation similar to the one he himself offered for the defense of Nazism in his literary debate with James Gallagher (see chapter four). Yet as S.R. Wilson points out in his review of the novel (*"La cabeza de la hidra," Journal of Spanish Studies, Twentieth Century* (1979):107–10):

> Every Jew in the novel is a spy for Israel. Every Jew is a Mexican national and an Israeli agent; every Jew is willing to sell land and information about Mexico to further the domination and control of the New York-Tel Aviv link. . . . Jewish women abound in the novel; they all betray. Sara Klein . . . is unblemished because she falls in love with a young Palestinian when she is abruptly murdered by Israeli agents. The only good Jew, therefore, is the one who concedes historical and territorial rights of the Palestinian people in the Middle East. The others are grotesque caricatures of *provocateurs*, exploiters, drug-dealers, and whores; all closely linked to Zionism, the Irgun, and Israeli detention centers.

Wilson contends that Fuentes's absorption in the Palestinian question is irrelevant to the development of the novel; that he injects his interpretation of Middle Eastern policy into the novel in "an attempt to justify the desire of the Palestinian to reclaim his homeland" (p. 110).

If this indeed were the case, it would indicate that Fuentes has not yet given up on the Mexican, anti-Zionist, Marxist youth who applauded him some twenty years ago; that this novel marks a return to realism in literature and increasing leftism in the political spectrum.

Nevertheless, Wilson's interpretation is far from totally convincing. In my own opinion, the Palestinian issue cannot be ignored in any discussion, fictional or otherwise, of the situation in the Middle East. It is a natural component of the plot of *The Hydra Head*. And since all characters in the novel are essentially caricatures, there is no reason for Fuentes to treat his Jewish marionettes any differently from the others. In contrast to Wilson, I do not believe that Fuentes takes any part of his spy thriller very seriously. He plays with the ideology of conflicting nationalisms just as he plays with the pretensions of international espionage. And although his dialogues are essentially Fuentes debating with Fuentes, there are several passages reminiscent of Arthur Koestler's *Darkness at Noon*, and which should at least prove interesting for students of Middle Eastern politics. Here once more is Fuentes, the journalist, offering us his insights into the contemporary world of international politics.

All this makes *The Hydra Head* faintly resemble Fuentes's earlier excursions into realism such as *Where the Air Is Clear*, and particularly *The Good Conscience*. Like them, it deals on the factual level with a recognizable society. Does *The Hydra Head* then portend that Fuentes is shifting into reverse gear, getting ready to return to something like this earlier period in his literary development? Possibly, but this work, like most of Fuentes's previous production, transmits a variety of conflicting messages. Billed as a "spy thriller," it is nevertheless fitted out with a mythological title. And this title is not mere ornamentation, but is fundamental to Fuentes's metaphysical conception of the novel.

The Mythological Theme

Although *The Hydra Head* would gain in popular appeal if we could identify with the protagonist and condemn his enemies, Fuentes, perhaps to his credit, attempts nothing of the sort. As usual, he straddles the line between frank commercialism and his own brand of didacticism. He reminds us again that evil cannot be confined to single characters and excluded from his heroes. Just as he showed us that the witch was innocent (as well as guilty) in *Holy Place*, and that Nazis could marshal strong arguments to support their actions in *Change of Skin*, in *The Hydra Head* he gives us little to choose from (in my opinion) between agents of the KGB, the CIA, the Arabs, or the infant Mexican organization. They are all different heads of the same Hydra, who, in Fuentes's version of the myth, can never be destroyed. In attempting to destroy evil, we merely assure its proliferation. The tragedy is perpetual and inevitable since it lies in the human psyche, particularly in human passion. The "brains" of the Mexican organization, Fuentes's narrator and alterego, says: "Ah, passion again rears its fearful Hydra Head. Cut off one, and a thousand grow in its place . . . " (p. 244). As in *Terra Nostra*, we witness Fuentes's obsession with the tenets of Gnosticism, particularly the horror of dissolution and multiplicity. If there is one villain, it is passion.

Trevor/Mann, the Wise Old Man

Trevor/Mann, the Mexican double agent and narrator, represents the cool, logical brain who dominates his passionate antagonists through his own cultivated aloofness. He is the new counterpart of Herr Urs of *Change of Skin*. Trevor is also like Felipe in *Terra Nostra*, who could disguise himself and betray friends with equanimity. Trevor, too, controls his own passions, all in the interest of a higher cause. Like Felipe, he is pictured as a devout Catholic: "I'm a Catholic, Félix, I know that when one lacks passion he can be saved by grace" (p. 245).

Yet Trevor, for all his boasted coldness, harbors a homosexual passion for Félix. (Now we understand how Félix got his job.) And this leads to the same kind of love-hate physical struggle that took place between Javier and Franz in the pyramid of *Change of Skin*. The cold super-spy (who can never come in from the cold because he incarnates it) turns out to have an Achilles' heel of passion: "my brother, my enemy, whom I finally held in an embrace of hatred, a struggle in which the bodies that had never touched in the sofa bed in New York were now locked together in rage . . . " (p. 245). As any veteran reader of Fuentes may remember, *Holy Place* also utilized the theme of the love-hate relationship between brothers.

In Fuentes's novelistic world, the same archetypal characters and situations appear again and again. Names, sometimes even sexes, change, but basic motivations of character remain the same. Trevor/Mann says of Maldonado: "I wanted him to love me, but I wanted him to fear me more" (p. 246). We need only compare this statement to that of "Mito" in *Holy Place* when he describes his mother, Claudia Nervo: "Known for her beauty, the Medusa demands to be recognized for her horror" (p. 120). Both Trevor and Claudia represent herculean attempts to shake off Mexican sentimentality and to emerge as semidivine figures. Claudia, too, we may remember, is notable for her Mexican chauvinism and her masculine traits. Trevor is a closet homosexual who suppresses his (feminine) feelings in the cause of superpatriotism. Yet both he and Claudia fail to dominate their emotions completely. Lanin Gyurko, who has written numerous articles of criticism on Fuentes, confirms this: "Despite her vehement declaration of androgyny, Claudia is vulnerable to male influence. Her tragic flaw is her narcissism."[3]

Trevor, too, in spite of himself, makes the mistake of caring for Félix and exposing himself to pain: "Félix defended himself against the aggression of my love coldly, the way someone defends himself against a mosquito" (p. 246). Trevor's lapse into passion predictably results in emotional wounds.

To put matters bluntly, Fuentes has a repertory of stock characters who are more or less interchangeable, even sexually. Rather than people observed with all their particular idiosyncracies and life experiences, they are fleshed-out aspects of Fuentes's own psyche—incarnations of narcissism, love of power, self-doubt, metaphysical yearnings, etc. They are unintegrated parts of a single personality projected by Fuentes, as writer, into the outside world where they appear as many characters. The horror of diversity and multiplication of the species that we find in *Terra Nostra* and *The Hydra Head* is a reflection of the horror of the fractionalized personality confronted with the constant love-hate relationship between elements within himself. In *Terra Nostra* an artificial integration is provided, premised on the notion that one solution lies in sex. But the euphoria of the sexual solution is only temporary.

In *The Hydra Head*, the unity which Fuentes had postulated through an androgynous solution in *Terra Nostra* again becomes his preoccupation. The violent passions which give birth to the Hydra can only be repressed temporarily, not integrated into the self. If we consider *The Hydra Head* as a serious book, it follows the tradition of all his previous novels in its message of Mexican fatalism.

The Snare of Sex in Fuentes's Works

One of the problems in Fuentes's novels is that in his trajectory from witch to androgyne he never really gets beyond the stage of hermaphroditism. He always falls back into the snare of sex, much as his hero Maldonado never reaches his goal of fusing spiritual love and physical love in his relationship with Sara. There is always a femme fatale, like Mary, to interpose herself. Just as Richard Callan notes in his discussion of *Aura*: "Sexuality is only one of the regressive forces and should be understood symbolically . . . "[4]

Perhaps that is why there is an air of abnormality in Fuentes's erotic scenes, an aura of guilt or depravity. This is also pointed out by Linda Hall: "For Fuentes, love is abnormal, a violation of the innocence of man. His stories are filled with incestuous unions or the desire for them—with mother, aunt, with pubescent nephew, brother with sister—with endless reworkings . . . and woman is always the corrupter."[5] The Ulysses of Fuentes's unconscious is mesmerized by the siren song of the witch, of Circe, and never completes its journey. Like Félix Maldonado, most of Fuentes's male protagonists are weak, easy prey for the devouring female. The unconscious is magnetized by the femme fatale or the devouring mother figure, and gropes ineffectually for the inspiration and transformation that the anima could also provide. Most of Fuentes's protagonists, therefore, are on a treadmill, condemned to the same frustrating role from novel to novel.[6]

Fuentes's Fatalism

His fatalistic message has much in common with that of Octavio Paz, Juan Rulfo, and Azuela, to mention only other Mexican writers. But the fatalistic tradition is widespread, with deep historic roots in Peninsular Spanish literature as well. And as we originally noted, even in the works of Lope de Vega, the witch appears as a harbinger of fate. Going back still further, Luis Vives, the great humanist and scholar of the early sixteenth century who was considered a feminist for his time, wrote that, "all the good and evil which is done in the world can be said without equivocation to be caused by women."[7]

Fuentes's domination by the female archetype of fate, therefore, is neither original nor surprising. The revolutionary aspect of his work lies basically in the literary devices he employs and combines—in technique, rather than in theme. He is revolutionary only in the generic sense, that he would carry us back full circle to the earliest period in literature, to a time of tales told about mythical heroes and supernatural beings. And, as we have seen in our analysis of his latest spy thriller, even supposedly realistic works are impregnated with mythical allusions and assumptions.

As Fuentes has clearly shown in *Terra Nostra* and repeated in essay after essay, his goal is to abolish time and history. Yet even *Terra Nostra* is a historically oriented escape. He does not abolish history so much as create a new metahistory, one in which space replaces time. (This phenomenon is discussed in general terms by Paul Tillich in *The Protestant Era*. Tillich points out that one of the major premises of the nonhistorical interpretation of history is that space is predominant against time; time is considered to be circular, or repeating itself infinitely. From this it follows that salvation is the salvation of individuals from time and history—the conclusion of *Terra Nostra*—rather than the salvation of the community through time and history, and that history is understood as a process of deterioration leading to the inescapable destruction of the world era.)[8]

The Danger of Timelessness

This attitude, as Philip Rahv points out in *Literature and the Sixth Sense,* is fraught with danger. He warns: "In literature the withdrawal from historic experience and creativeness can only mean stagnation. For the creative artist to deny time in the name of timelessness is to misconceive his task. He will never discover a shortcut to transcendence. . . . The critics captivated by this procedure [the search for the mythic model] are inclined to take for granted that to identify a mythic pattern in a novel or poem is tantamount to disclosing its merit—an assumption patently false. . . . What is not grasped . . . is that timelessness is in itself nothing more than a pledge waiting for time to redeem it. . . ."[9]

Rahv does not mention Fuentes, but the relevance of his statement for Fuentes's works is immediately apparent. We may remember that at least since 1966 Fuentes has considered the mythical alternative as the only alternative for the Latin American writer, as the one providing him "a chance to leave that past which is only history, stray history, in order to begin a dialectic, which is to create history and to create it out of myths."[10] This has been Fuentes's preoccupation as novelist and playwright for a decade and a half. *Change of Skin, Cumpleaños,* and *Terra Nostra* all substitute myth for history, while *The Hydra Head* superimposes a mythical pattern on the chaos of contemporary world politics. Yet Fuentes does not succeed in abolishing history or time, at least not for the reader. Nearly every critic, for example, makes a point of the enormous investment in time necessary to read his latest works (excluding *The Hydra Head,* of course). Rather than dissolving time, he makes us increasingly aware of its existence.

Other Problems in the Mythical Approach

There are other problems that both average reader and critic experience with the mythical approach, at least the approach as perceived by Fuentes. Fuentes's myths are only for the select, the initiate. The myths that children hear as fairy tales and that primitive peoples pass on through oral tradition concern themselves with great heroes, with whom the listener can identify in an experience that truly dissolves time. Yet the labyrinthine structures that Fuentes creates contain none of the super-heroes of primitive myth. In theme, they are closer to what Max Lüthi would call a "local legend." These, unlike fairy tales, "provide no answer to existential questions but express the anxiety of man who, although apparently a part of the community of fellow men, finds himself ultimately confronted with an uncanny world . . . which threatens him with death. It portrays man as unblessed, unsuccessful, facing life's ultimate questions alone and uncertain." The characters in these anti–fairy tales, like those in the genuine article, "are not primarily individuals, but simply figures: doers and receivers of action."[11]

The Genuine Fairy Tale

Yet the genuine fairy tale "appeals to the listener's feeling for form, his ability to visualize, his sense of rhythm and even his humor. It portrays essential processes of life: testing, threatening danger, destruction—and salvation, development and maturation."[12] It leaves us with a feeling of elation totally at odds with the Kafkian treatment so popular with Fuentes and other writers of our day. Fuentes's characters, as we have seen, seldom mature, but almost invariably regress to a state of preconsciousness before the emergence of ego. Furthermore, even the inherent drama that might be elicited from this tragedy is muted by the excessive intellectualization of the process. The fact is that Fuentes's sophisticated readers are trying to unravel the puzzle he presents by recourse to their powers of deduction, memory, and education. They are trying to understand what he is saying, not to experience or feel it. None of the psychological requirements for the receptiveness to myth are present. Today, perhaps the only mythmaker in the ancient tradition is Tolkien.

In fairy-tale language, we should like to see Fuentes's witch outwitted by a wise sorceress or a beautiful princess who would afterwards marry the slayer of dragons and witches. We should like to witness the drama of one successful battle against the witch. But she is always there, hovering in the background, even in such semi-realistic works as *The Hydra Head.* She always manages to get her way in Fuentes's insistence on fate and futility. Furthermore, she can brook no rivals and, as we saw in *The Hydra Head,* makes sure to kill off poor Sara, who was perhaps Fuentes's best hope for the androgynous solution he had been dreaming of since *Holy Place.*

Yet long, long ago, before the witch overpowered his unconscious and polluted the clear air of Mexico City with the smoke of witches burning and being burned, there were real characters and real dramatic tension in Fuentes's works. Even in *Aura,* the witch intrudes cautiously upon an essentially realistic stage, thus producing a genuine gothic novel. The occult here could still cause shivers because it was inserted into a familiar setting. But as Fuentes surrendered to the dictates of the unconscious, his novels have acquired the character of monologues, with the author manipulating each character-puppet. Characters speak because Fuentes requires them to express certain ideas. Dialogue is imposed by an author-narrator who, no matter how protean, always betrays himself as Fuentes. Even *The Hydra Head* is action built around words, not the reverse.

Yet this was not always so. Fuentes is perfectly capable of creating, or at least of suggesting, real characters. Often it is his less ambitious works which are his most successful in this respect. When he resists his impulse for fresco painting and tosses off a quick pen and ink sketch, he reveals his talent for true character portrayal. Specifically, I am thinking now of his short stories, of such masterpieces as "La Vieja Moralidad" ("The Old Morality"), or "La Muñeca Reina" ("The Doll Queen") of his *Cantar de ciegos (Song of the Blind.)*[13] The explanation for the success of these stories is not the absence of the anima figure. In "The Old Morality" she is present in the sexually frustrated aunt who almost unconsciously tries to seduce her pubescent nephew. And in "The Doll Queen" she is again present in the crippled and mentally retarded young woman rejected by her own parents in favor of a doll within a coffin, an image of the woman as a beautiful child. The drama of these stories lies in the resistance of the narrator to the menacing female. In "The Old Morality" he is intuitively aware of the danger represented by the aunt, and seeks to avoid it. In "The Doll Queen" he is nauseated by the parents' necrophilic worship, and when finally confronted with the real and monstrous grown woman, he does not enter the house. The anima figure in its youthful and mysterious form inspires the story. But when it metamorphoses into witch, he retreats into the everyday world of rain and reality, rather than the cloying warmth of the unconscious.

It is interesting that this story duplicates the archetypal experience related by Fuentes in his letter of December 1968, his already mentioned encounter as a boy with the representation of the empress Carlota as a young beauty, and then as a dead old woman in her coffin. (Here, of course, the representations are reversed chronologically as he goes from a dead child represented in a coffin to a live, but horrible woman.) But his own interpretation of the Carlota experience is equally applicable to "The Doll Queen." As he says in his letter: "It is all a part of our history and our life: the history of everything that cannot die because it has never lived."

The monstrous woman of "The Doll Queen" cannot die—in spite of her parents' effigy—because her spirit, her anima, has never lived. Treated as a short story, the theme is evocative and haunting. Its grounding in sensual and earthy details makes it bloom in our imaginations. Furthermore, Fuentes gives each reader the liberty to end the story according to his own feelings. The front door remains open. The hero could go back another time, and discover that there is beauty of soul hidden beneath the crippled exterior of Amilamia. Or he may see, as he stands in the pouring rain, that Amilamia is corrupt in body and soul alike.

In his short stories, Fuentes gives his characters—and his readers—room to breathe. The anima inspires, but does not stifle. This may be because she appears to pass quickly from Fuentes's unconscious to the printed page. She is not exposed to the light of day which is Fuentes's reason, not allowed to ferment there and grow out of proportion. It is precisely when Fuentes self-consciously manipulates the anima that she turns the tables and manipulates him. Thus Fuentes's more ambitious mythological works tend to become sterile exercises in a didacticism which would be better left in the essays where they first appear.

In short, we may say that Fuentes, obsessed by the anima since childhood, has been projecting her both consciously and unconsciouly into his fictional works. When the effort is conscious, the anima rebels and smothers his creation. But when she enters behind his back, disguising herself as a minor character of a novel (Ludivinia of *Artemio Cruz,* or Mercedes of *Where the Air Is Clear*), or when she is at least disciplined by the limitations of space, the effect can be haunting and emotional, in the original tradition of myth.

Appendix

Mexico City, July 24th., 1969
Dear Gloria Durán:

I know I'm late in answering your letter of May 29; please excuse me; please try to imagine what it means to re-enter "la región más turbia del aire" after four years in Europe, especially when my poor country is in the midst of a fascistic repression against students, intellectuals and all independently minded people.

I'll try to answer your questions. But first of all, I'd like to ask YOU a favour. Next year, Ediciones Era is publishing a big, highly-priced book of mine called LAS VIEJAS. It is actually an anthology of my witches, and includes "Tlactocatzine", "El muñeco", "Aura", chapters from "La Región" (Teódula) and from "Cruz" (Ludivinia), as well as an unpublished fragment, "Noticia necrológica", in which an ubiquitous sorceress plays at the same time, with two men who might be one, in a Veracruz jungle today and on a Castillian road in the XVIth. century. The book will be fully illustrated by Cuevas. My publishers and I thought it would be a great idea if we also included, as a preface, a 20-page synthesis of your ideas on the subject. Would you be amenable?

1. I confess: I have not read Jung. My intuition of the mythical must be a priori; a posteriori, any ideas I now have about the subject are very much due to Lévi-Strauss: the myth as a perpetual present, the myth as itself plus all the commentaries it has provoked, myth as a chain of reflections, myth as the oldest social discourse between body and soul, living and dead, remembered and foreseen, etc.

2. The clues to the narrator in Cambio de piel are several. One is Xipe Totec, the flayed one: renewal and sacrifice. The other is the narrator's own name: Freddy Lambert. Freddy, from Nietzsche; Lambert, from the Balzac character, Louis Lambert. Both—the philosopher and the personaje—were first Melmoth the Wanderer, Maturin's character of 1821 (?): a man whose organs are no longer capable of sustaining his thought. You will remember that Lambert is secluded in a house that is more like a hospital or a lunatic asylum; there, he sits in darkness and thinks: he cannot communicate his thoughts any more, since they are so frightfully clear and quick; velocity of thought makes him pass as an idiot. And so ended Nietzsche. Yes, I'm interested in FN* the way Klossowsky explains him: nature cannot be known and thought of at the same time; furthermore, the objective structure of nature cannot be thought of without going mad. All this ought to be translated to Freddy Lambert's thought and knowledge of a total novel.

3. The best piece on Zona Sagrada was published by François Bott in Le Monde, issue of August 10, 1968. It is reproduced in the 4th. spanish edition as a postface. Your interpretations sound very, very valid.

*Friedrich Nietzsche

4. Yes, both Ixca and Freddy could be considered male witches. But the male strain, as you so very well observe, is on gnosis, and gnosis is activism, vs. the passive knowledge of the female witches.

5. The phrase from Los días enmascarados was the one written on mantas and with flowers in arches on the arrival of Maximilian and Charlotte in Mexico. The exact meaning is translated in Bertita Harding's "Phantom Crown". Tlactocatzine means "Lord" or "Emperor".

You'll be receiving my booklet on the contemporary Spanish American novel in a few weeks. Do write at once on the Era proposal. All best to you and Manolo from you friend, Carlos.

Carlos

París, 8 de diciembre de 1968

Querida Gloria Durán:

Muchas gracias por su amable carta del 19 de noviembre. Perdone el retraso en contestarle: estaba en Barcelona, recibiendo a nuestro amigo Octavio Paz que, como usted sabe, renunció a su embajada en la India cuando, precisamente, ese subconsciente colectivo del que usted habla resurgió en la mal llamada Plaza de las Tres Culturas.

Recuerda usted que cuando le preguntaron a Alfonso Reyes si podía detectar las influencias literarias en Rulfo y Arreola, don Alfonso contestó: "Sí, dos mil años de literatura". Claro, la señora Borderau y la Condesa Ranevskaya (cuántas veces no habré visto aquella magnífica película de Thororld Dickinson con Dame Edith Evans!); pero también la Miss Havisham de Dickens, la figura arquetípica de la bruja de Michelet, las viejas (para limitarnos esta vez a Latinoamérica) de Bianco y Donoso ("Sombras suele vestir" y "Coronación"). En fin: se podría trazar un antiquísimo linaje. Pero si no salimos de mi propia obra, verá usted que existe esa obsesión con lo que Octavio llama "la encantadora, la bruja, la serpiente blanca", primero en mi cuento "Tlactocatzine, del Jardín de Flandes" (la vieja y loca Emperatriz Carlota), luego en "La región más transparente" (la anciana hechicera, Tonantzin desplazada a las vecindades, Teódula Moctezuma) y, al tiempo que escribia "Aura", en el personaje de la vieja Ludivinia, encerrada en el único cuarto de un casco incendiado, en "La muerte de Artemio Cruz". Pero si le soy totalmente franco, esa obsesión nació en mí cuando tenía siete años y, después de visitar el castillo de Chapultepec y ver el cuadro de la joven Carlota de Bélgica, encontré en el archivo Casasola la fotografía de esa misma mujer, ahora vieja, muerta, recostada dentro de un féretro acojinado, tocada con una cofia de niña: la Carlota que murió, loca, en un castillo, el mismo año en que yo nací. Las dos Carlotas: Aura y Consuelo. Quizás Carlota nunca supo que envejecía. Hasta el fin le escribía cartas de amor a Maximiliano. Correspondencia entre fantasmas. Es toda una parte de nuestra historia y de nuestra vida: la historia de todo lo que no puede morir porque jamás ha vivido.

Bueno: no hay literatura huérfana, por más que los malos críticos de nuestros países así lo exijan ("el que lee a

Proust se proustituye", decía un beato chovinista literario en México). Y quizás no hay más novedad que las nuevas, y a veces escandalosas, combinaciones de la tradición. Una vez ví la "Medea" de Séneca en una aldea de campesinos cerca de México, D.F. Los lugareños lloraban y gritaban de horror. Decían que era la historia de Doña Chonita que había matado a todos sus hijos. Otros, capaces de recordar el mito, decían que era la historia de "La Llorona". En otras palabras: la Emperatriz Carlota murió sin haber visto la imagen de la Condesa Ranevskaya interpretada por Edith Evans. Yo ví esa imagen y la de la propia Carlota muerta.

Ojalá que esto le sirva. Abrazos grandes a Manolo y a Emir. Para usted, el afecto de

Carlos

Notes

Introduction

1. Carlos Fuentes, "La situación del escritor en América Latina," *Mundo Nuevo* 1 (1966): 15
2. *Octavio Paz, The Labyrinth of Solitude*, Trans. Lysander Kemp (New York: Grove Press, 1961), p. 28.
3. For a full discussion of the foregoing, see chapter two.
4. Joseph Sommers, "The Present Moment in the Mexican Novel," *Books Abroad* 40 (1966): 263.
5. See letter from Fuentes to Durán, 8 December 1968, published in the Appendix.
6. "Carlos Fuentes et les Sorcières," *Le Figaro Littéraire*, 30 January 1964, p. 2.

Chapter I

1. Julio Caro-Baroja in *Vidas Mágicas e Inquisición* (Madrid: Taurus, 1967) also discusses less well-known Celestinas such as *La Celestina* of Juan Navarro de Espinosa, an *entremés* (interlude) published in 1643 (vol. 1, p. 117). On pages 119–20 he deals with Cervantes' witches as well, and also those of Lope de Vega.
2. William McCreary, *The Goldfinch and the Hawk*, (Chapel Hill: University of North Carolina Press, 1966), pp. 53–56.
3. Ibid., p. 58.
4. Andrew M. Greeley, "There's a New Time Religion on Campus," *New York Times Magazine*, 1 June 1969, p. 14.
5. Ibid., p. 27.

6. Carl G. Jung, *Psychology and Religion,* (New Haven: Yale University Press, 1938), p. 64.

7. Douglas Hill and Pat Williams, *The Supernatural* (New York: Hawthorne Books, 1965), p. 174.

8. Although the anima is treated in many of Jung's works—for example, in *The Integration of the Personality* (with its chapter three on "Archetypes of the Collective Unconscious"), and in *Psychology and Religion* (with particular reference to part two, "Dogma and Natural Symbols")—it is perhaps given most extensive treatment in *The Archetypes and the Collective Unconscious* (New York: Pantheon Books, 1959).

9. Carl G. Jung, *The Integration of the Personality,* (New York: Farrar and Reinhart, 1939), p. 18.

10. Ibid., pp. 22, 23.

11. Carl G. Jung, "The Psychological Aspects of the Kore," in *Essays on a Science of Mythology* with Carl Kerényi, Bollingen Series, XXII (Princeton: Princeton University Press, 1969), p. 173.

12. Carl G. Jung, "The Psychology of the Child Archetype," in *Essays on a Science . . .,* p. 72.

13. Jung, *Psychology and Religion,* p. 63.

14. Ibid., p. 64.

15. Claude Lévi-Strauss, *Anthropologie Structurale* (Paris: Plon, 1958), p. 230.

16. Northrop Frye, *Anatomy of Criticism* (New York: Atheneum, 1969), p. 291.

17. Gerald Sykes, *The Hidden Remnant* (New York: Harper, 1962), p. 34.

18. "The Square of the Three Cultures" is so named because of its vestige of a pyramid, a baroque church, and a modern skyscraper—in short, the three cultures that coexist in modern Mexico.

19. Jung, *Psychology and Religion,* p. 17.

20. Ibid., p. 64.

21. Lionel Trilling, "Art and Neurosis," in *Art and Psychoanalysis,* ed. William Phillips (New York: World, 1957), quoted in Sykes, *The Hidden Remnant,* p. 165.

22. Ibid., p. 9.

23. Quoted by Joseph Sommers, *After the Storm,* (Albuquerque, N.M.: U. of New Mexico Press, 1968), p. 96.

24. Quoted by Sykes, *The Hidden Remnant,* p. 166.

25. Carlos Fuentes, "La situación del escritor en América Latina," *Mundo Nuevo* 1 (1966): 13.

26. Frye, *Anatomy of Criticism*, p. 186.

27. Ibid.

28. These are elements mentioned by Frye (Anatomy of Criticism, p. 238) as "typical of the final stage of comedy." The "gothic romance" can be exemplified in *Aura*; the myth of the return to the womb in *Holy Place*; the imaginative withdrawal in *Change of Skin*.

Chapter II

1. As Leon Edel points out, the inspiration for James was a real person, a famous actress who had been mistress of Byron, and the story related in *The Aspern Papers* was based on an anecdote told him by a friend. See Edel, *The Middle Years* (Englewood Cliffs: Prentice-Hall, 1963), pp. 218, 219.

2. Gloria B. Durán, "El problema de la imitación y la inspiración en *La Dama de Espadas, Los papeles de Aspern y Aura*" (unpublished manuscript).

3. Carl G. Jung, *The Archetypes and the Collective Unconscious*, (New York: Pantheon Books, 1959), p. 71.

4. Joseph Sommers, *After the Storm*, (Albuquerque, N.M.: U. of New Mexico Press, 1968), p. 181.

5. Joseph Sommers, "The Present Moment in the Mexican Novel," *Books Abroad*, 40 (1966): 262.

6. Robert Mead, Jr., "Carlos Fuentes, Mexico's Angry Novelist," *Books Abroad* 38 (1964): 262.

7. Carlos Fuentes, *Los dias enmascarados (The Masked Days)*, (Mexico: D.F. Novaro, S.A., 1966), p. 44.

8. Fuentes's birth date, which is something of a mystery, is usually given as 1928 or 1929. Yet according to the *Gran Enciclopedia Larousse*, (Spanish edition of 1967), Carlota died in 1927. By adding an extra year or two to his age (a surprising gesture in our youth-oriented author), Fuentes seems to be indulging in poetic license in order, like Henry James, to reinforce his intimacy or even identity, with the anima figure.

9. Carl G. Jung, "The Psychology of the Child Archetype," in *Essays on a Science of Mythology* with Carl Kerényi: Bollingen Series, XXII (Princeton: Princeton University Press, 1969), p. 99.

10. Luis Harss and Barbara Dohmann, *Into the Mainstream* (New York: Harper and Row, 1967), p. 302.

11. Ibid., p. 19.

12. Mead, "Carlos Fuentes," p. 380.

13. Sommers, "The Present Moment," p. 262.

14. Quoted in Sommers, *After the Storm*, p. 180.

15. Carlos Fuentes, *Aura*, trans. Lysander Kemp (New York: Farrar, Straus and Giroux, 1965). Please note that the translations as given here are my own.

16. Mead, "Carlos Fuentes," p. 382.

17. In the original Spanish edition (Mexico, D.F.: Era, 1962), this section is found on page 60.

18. Octavio Paz, *The Labyrinth of Solitude*, trans. Lysander Kemp (New York: Grove Press, 1961), pp. 196, 197.

19. The influence of Paz on Fuentes has been so well identified by the critics—e.g. see Sommers's *After the Storm*, pp. 127, 132—and in the frequent references to Paz by Fuentes himself—see Fuentes to Durán, 8 December 1968 in the Appendix—that it requires no demonstration.

20. Sommers, *After the Storm*, p. 179.

21. Andrew M. Greeley, "There's a New Time Religion on Campus," *New York Times Magazine*, 1 June 1969, p. 24.

22. Ibid., p. 33.

23. Harss and Dohmann, *Into the Mainstream*, p. 302.

24. Douglas Hill and Pat Williams, *The Supernatural* (New York: Hawthorne Books, 1965), p. 198.

25. Ibid., p. 179.

26. Ibid., p. 180. Even as late as the mid-seventeenth century, we are told by Julio Caro-Baroja (*Vidas mágicas e Inquisición* [Madrid: Taurus, 1967], vol. 1, p. 125) that "sorceresses were punished by sentences that in reality did not correspond to the gravity of the crimes they were accused of . . ." And he asks: "How could it be that a pact with the Devil was considered less serious than the act of obeying some Hebrew law? The answer is simple: In reality this pact was always considered to be a bit of a fraud."

27. Ibid., p. 180.

28. See Ibid., p. 210.

29. Ibid., p. 211.

30. Richard Callan, "The Jungian Basis of Carlos Fuentes' 'Aura,'" *Kentucky Romance Quarterly* 18 (1971): 67.

31. Harss and Dohmann, *Into the Mainstream*, p. 302.

32. René Dubos, "Biological Individuality," *Columbia Forum* 12 (Spring, 1969): 5.

33. Jung, *The Archetypes and the Collective Unconscious*, p. 118.

34. Paz, *The Labyrinth*, p. 210.

35. Ibid., p. 198.

36. Callan, "The Jungian Basis . . ." p. 73.

37. Fuentes discusses the German writer's profound influence on his thoughts in an interview with Jose Miguel Ullán in *Insula* 22 (1967): 1, 12–13. We may remember that Nietzsche stated that "the past and the present are one and the same, typically alike in all their diversity, and forming together a picture of eternally present, imperishable types of unchangeable value and significance." (This statement quoted from *The Use and Abuse of History* and is reprinted on page 223 of Geoffrey Clive's *The Philosophy of Nietzsche* [New York: Mentor, 1965].)

38. This style may in part be inspired by D. H. Lawrence in whose works, according to Fuentes, "you find a tone of prophetic imminence. He is always on the brink of the future, it is always there, latent" (quoted by Harss and Dohmann, *Into the Mainstream*, p. 295).

39. My only serious disagreement with Callan's excellent article lies in his final supposition that Fuentes deliberately adapted and transposed "into his tight little case history as many facets as possible of *Symbols of Transformation* and like Jungian studies" (Callan, "The Jungian Basis . . ." p. 75). To accept this hypothesis is, in any case, a denial of Fuentes's own statement that he was unacquainted with Jung (a statement of which Callan was probably not aware or disbelieved). However, since the same archetypal situation occurs in *Los dias enmascarados*, Callan must also assume that Fuentes was conversant with Jung in his early twenties (long before Jung became fashionable in Mexico).

40. Jung, *The Archetypes and the Collective Unconscious*, p. 26.

41. Carlos Fuentes, *The Death of Artemio Cruz*, trans. Sam Hileman (New York: Farrar, Straus and Giroux, 1964), p. 285.

42. "Carlos Fuentes et les Sorcières," *Le Figaro Littéraire*, 30 January 1964, p. 2.

43. Carlos Fuentes, *Where the Air Is Clear*, trans. Sam Hileman (New York: Farrar, Straus and Giroux, 1960), p. 269.

44. Alfonso Caso, *La religión de los Aztecas* (Mexico, D.F.: 1945), p. 45.

45. Rivkah Schärf Kluger, *Satan and the Old Testament* (Evanston, Illinois: Northwestern University Press, 1967), p. 42.

46. This is a literal translation of page 409 of the original Spanish version (Mexico, D.F.: Fondo de Cultura Económica, 1958). The English version translated by Sam Hileman does not make the point so clearly, but may be found on page 331.

47. Understood in this light, Hortensia is far from "an object of her master's greedy passion for luxury items," as Harss and Dohmann describe her (*Into the Mainstream*, p. 287.).

48. Hill and Williams, *The Supernatural*, p. 157.

49. Ibid.

50. Ibid., p. 228.

51. Ibid., p. 229.

52. Ibid., p. 225.

Chapter III

1. Carlos Fuentes, "La situación del escritor en América Latina, *Mundo Nuevo* I (1966): 15.

2. Robert Graves, *The Greek Myths,* (Baltimore: Pelican Books, 1966), 2: 373.

3. Fuentes, "La situación," p. 15.

4. Carlos Fuentes, *Holy Place*, trans. Susanne Jill Levine (New York: Dutton, 1972), p. 13.

5. Franz Kafka, "The Silence of the Sirens," in *Homer, a Collection of Critical Essays*, ed. George Steiner, (Englewood Cliffs, N.J.: Prentice-Hall, 1962), p. 96.

6. Robert Graves, "Ulysses," *Homer, a Collection*, p. 139.

7. For further confirmation of this thesis with respect to the identity of Claudia, see the article by François Bott in *Le Monde*, 10 August 1968, an article that Fuentes recommended to me as "the best piece on *Zona sagrada*" in his letter of 24 July 1969.

8. Carl G. Jung, *Psychology and Religion* (New Haven: Yale University Press, 1938), p. 34.

9. Northrop Frye, *Anatomy of Criticism* (New York: Atheneum, 1969), p. 149.

10. Severo Sarduy, "Un fetiche de cachemira," *Mundo Nuevo* 18 (1967):87.

11. Ibid., p. 87.

12. Ibid. Sarduy's reference to Claudia as "neutral" may perhaps suggest that she is androgynous, rather than hermaphroditic, as the term is explained by Mircea Eliade in his *Mephistopheles and the Androgyne* (New York: Sheed and Ward, 1965). For a further discussion of the distinction between these terms, please see chapter seven.

13. Ibid., p. 88.

14. Jung, *Psychology and Religion*, p. 69.

15. Octavio Paz, *The Labyrinth of Solitude*, trans. Lysander Kemp (New York: Grove Press, 1961), p. 93.

16. Ibid.

17. Ibid., p. 84. Here Paz interprets López Velarde, who says that " ⁶Cuahtémoc went out to meet Cortés—that is to say the final sacrifice—separated from the curved breast of the Empress.' "

18. Alfonso Caso, *La religión de los Aztecas* (Mexico, D. F.: Secretaría de Educación Pública, 1945), p. 26.

19. Paz, *The Labyrinth*, p. 127.

20. Ibid.

21. Caso, *La Religión*, p. 43.

22. Ibid., pp. 45, 47.

23. Ibid., p. 47.

24. Paz, *The Labyrinth*, see the chapter on "The Sons of La Malinche."

25. George McMurray, "Zona sagrada," *Books Abroad* 42, no. 1 (1968):82.

26. Mircea Eliade, *Mephistopheles and the Androgyne* (New York: Sheed and Ward, 1965), *passim*, especially pp. 103–111.

27. This reference to Pan is perhaps unfortunate for the symmetry of the myth since, according to Graves, some sources deny that Penelope was faithful to Ulysses: "They accuse her of companying with Amphinomus of Dulichium, or with all the suitors in turn and they say that the fruit of this union was the monstrous Pan, at sight of which Odysseus fled for shame to Aetolia . . ." (Graves, *The Greek Myths*, p. 373.) Thus Fuentes may be inadvertently suggesting that Giancarlo, alias Telemachus, was not really Ulysses's son in the first place.

28. It is not perhaps accurate to use the designation "Freudian" here since Jung has pointed out that Freud himself recognized that underlying the personal, mother-son relationship was an infantile preconception of the mother figure and that myth-forming structural elements must be present in the unconscious psyche. Carl G. Jung, "The Psychology of the Child Archetype," in *Essays on a Science of Mythology* with Carl Kerényi, Bollingen Series, XXII (Princeton: Princeton University Press, 1969), p. 71.

29. Carl G. Jung, "Ulysses, a Monologue," in *The Spirit in Man, Art and Literature, Collected Works*, vol. 15, Bollingen Series, XX, (Princeton: Princeton University Press, 1966), *passim*. "Ulysses" was written in 1932.

30. Ibid.

31. Frye, *Anatomy of Criticism*, p. 148.

32. It is interesting to note that Eliade (*Mephistopheles and the Androgyne*, p. 104) also points out that Adam, according to several *mishrashim*, was androgynous, and that Leone Ebreo has tried to connect, in his *Dialoghi d'Amore*, the Platonic myth of the Androgyne with the Biblical tradition of the Fall.

Chapter IV

1. Carlos Fuentes, "La situación del Escritor en América Latina," *Mundo Nuevo*, 1 (1966):15.

2. Joseph Sommers, "The present moment in the Mexican Novel," *Books Abroad*, 40 (1966): 261.

3. Ibid.

4. Carlos Fuentes, *Change of Skin*, trans. Sam Hileman (New York: Farrar, Straus and Giroux, 1967), p. 269.

5. Page 374 of the English version mistranslates page 367 of the Spanish original (Mexico, D.F.: Joaquín Mortiz, 1967) which says: "He [Javier] has spent his life inventing lies, obliging me to pretend in order to find out if his poor imagination would reawaken." The English version says: "He's spent his entire life playing let's-pretend games. They're not worth worrying about." Thus Elizabeth's role in Javier's games is ignored in the English translation.

6. Octavio Paz, *The Labyrinth of Solitude*, trans. Lysander Kemp (New York: Grove Press, 1961, p. 197.

7. In his excellent article "Freedom and Fate in Carlos Fuentes' *Cambio de Piel*," Lanin Gyurko discusses this stone serpent as symbolic of the closed, fatalistic world of the entire novel: "The cyclic time and circular space that characterize *Cambio de piel* . . . is vividly symbolized by the way in which the strangling serpent is evoked . . . For [Javier] the serpent is seen in terms of his personal life: it becomes the symbol of the destructive power of woman. He sees Elizabeth in profile, fused with the serpent, as she leans against the pyramid. His paranoic imagination links Elizabeth with the dread power of the god. (*Revista/Review Interamericana* 7, no. 4 [1977/78]: 708, 709.)

8. Northrop Frye, *Anatomy of Criticism*, (New York: Atheneum, 1969), p. 148.

9. I use the adjective *real* only in a very relative sense, for the purpose of classifying the characters according to some order. Perhaps the designation should be not in degrees of reality, but of fictionality, since as Andrés O. Avellaneda points out in "Función de la complejidad in *Cambio de piel* de Carlos Fuentes" (*Norte* X, no.

2 [1969]), p. 27: "*Cambio de piel* not only tells us that 'the only reality' that matters is false, but all its structure, its flesh and bones, create the kind of lack of restraint that protects this judgement."

10. Fuentes, "La situación del escritor," p. 11.

11. Ibid., p. 12.

12. Ibid.

13. Ibid., p. 10.

14. Quoted by Joseph Sommers, *After the Storm*, (Albuquerque, N.M.: U. of New Mexico Press, 1968), p. 135.

15. Marvin Harris, *Cows, Pigs, Wars and Witches* (New York: Random House, 1974), see especially pp. 238–39.

16. The charge does not emerge clearly in the review itself, "Stifled Tigers," *New York Times Book Review*, 5 February 1968, pp. 5, 40–41 but rather is implied in Gallagher's letter of self-defense answering Fuentes's attack on the review, both published 3 March 1968.

17. David Gallagher, "*A Change of Skin*," *New York Times*, 3 March 1968, section 7, p. 17.

18. Besides the author's conscious intent, some of the eloquence in the neo-Nazi passages of the book might well have been inspired by Jorge Luis Borges's short story "Deutsches Requiem" from *El Aleph*, (Buenos Aires: Emecé Editores S.A., 1962), with its terrifying defense of Nazism by an unrepentant ex-Nazi narrator. Brahms's "Deutsches Requiem" is also the thematic background in *Change of Skin* for the courtship between Franz and his condemned sweetheart.

19. José Miguel Ullán, "Carlos Fuentes, Salto Mortal Hacia Mañana," *Insula*, 22, no. 245 (1967):12.

20. Ibid.

21. Carlos Fuentes's "*A Change of Skin*," *New York Times*, 3 March 1968, section 7, p. 17.

22. Quoted by Ullán, "Carlos Fuentes," p. 12.

23. Cited by Geoffrey Clive, *The Philosophy of Nietzsche* (New York: Mentor, 1965), pp. 595, 596.

24. Carl G. Jung, *Psychology and Religion* (New Haven: Yale University Press, 1938), p. 33.

25. Douglas Hill and Pat Williams, (New York: Hawthorne Books, 1965), p. 334.

26. Marvin Harris, *Cows, Pigs, Wars and Witches* (New York: Random House, 1974), p. 258.

27. Carlos Fuentes, *Cambio de piel* (Mexico, D.F.: Joaquín Mortiz, 1967), pp. 416, 417.

28. Carl G. Jung, *The Archetypes and the Collective Unconscious* (New York: Pantheon Books, 1959), p. 37.

29. Ibid.

30. Jung, *Psychology and Religion*, p. 109.

31. Sydney H. Mellone, "Gnosticism," *Encyclopaedia Britannica*, 16th ed. 10:455.

32. Ibid.

33. Although a simplification, Lanin Gyurko's identification of him as a "Hitlerian symbol" is accurate. See "Freedom and Fate in Carlos Fuentes, *Cambio de Piel*," *Revista/Review Interamericana* 7, no. 4 [1977/78]:710.

34. According to Andrés O. Avellaneda, the rationale behind the entire complicated structure of the novel is based on the fullest possible application of this "mentira literaria"; it is the total fictionalization of the novel. See his "Función de la complejidad," p. 27.

35. Fuentes, *Cambio de piel*, p. 408. (I could not find this sentence in the English translation.) In spite of the "total fictionalization" of the novelistic form, the message that it contains is strongly reminiscent of the conventional, realistic novel of Pío Baroja, *El árbol de la ciencia*. Baroja, who was also strongly influenced by Nietzsche, affirms in the words of one of his characters: "The instinct for life requires fiction in order to affirm its existence." And to footnote his maxim in the Bible, he quotes Genesis: "You may eat all the fruits of the garden, but beware of the fruit of the tree of knowledge because the day that you eat of this fruit you will surely die." (*El arbol de la ciencia* [New York: Las Americas, 1957], p. 213).

36. The episode suggests the dilemma of the poet and the scientist who are asked to choose between atheism and superstition. As Francis Bacon pointed out, the scientist would be compelled to choose atheism, and the poet, superstition, "for even superstition, by its very confusion of values, gives his imagination more scope than a dogmatic denial of imaginative infinity does." (Cited by Frye, *Anatomy of Criticism*, p. 125.)

37. Ullán, "Carlos Fuentes," p. 13.

38. "Freddy from Nietzsche," he explains in the letter of 24 July 1969 included in the Appendix.

39. Gallagher, "Stifled Tiger," p. 5.

40. Fuentes, "La situación del escritor," p. 10.

41. Ibid., 14.

42. Sommers, *After the Storm*, pp. 108–30.

43. Gallagher, "Stifled Tiger," p. 5.

44. Or as Northrop Frye succinctly warns: "Culture interposes a total vision of possibilities . . . because whatever is excluded from culture by religion or state will get its revenge somehow." (*Anatomy of Criticism*, p. 127)

45. Dos Passos, Faulkner, and D.H. Lawrence are obviously influences in *Where the Air Is Clear;* Nietzsche, Balzac, and Cortázar in *Change of Skin.*

46. Gallagher, "Stifled Tiger," p. 41.

47. Raúl H. Castagnino, "Estado actual de la novela en Hispanoamérica," *Cuadernos del Sur,* 8–9 (1967–68):136. This article is extremely interesting in that it examines Fuentes and his Latin American fellow writers from a generational viewpoint very similar to that expressed by José Juan Arrom in his *Esquema Generacional de las letras hispanoamericanas* (Bogota: Instituto Caro y Cuervo, 1963), a viewpoint which has the advantage of relating our author to his contemporary cultural framework and which shows him to be, even as innovator, typical of his generation.

48. Castagnino, "Estado actual," p. 136.

49. Fuentes, "La situación del escritor," p. 10.

50. Ibid.

51. Frye, *Anatomy of Criticism*, p. 118.

52. Ibid., p. 122.

53. Ibid., pp. 124, 125.

54. Ibid., p. 135.

55. Ibid., p. 291.

56. Ibid.

57. Ibid.

58. Ibid.

59. Ibid.

60. Ibid., pp. 108, 110, 112.

Chapter V

1. We may remember that cats also played a significant role in the magical powers of Consuelo of *Aura.*

2. All references to *Cumpleaños (Birthday)* are to the first edition (Mexico, D.F.: Joaquín Mortiz, 1969).

3. Erich Neumann, *The Great Mother,* Bollingen Series, XLVII (Princeton: Princeton University Press, 1970), p. 170.

4. Carl Kerényi and Carl G. Jung, "The Primordial Child in Primordial Times," in *Essays on a Science of Mythology*, Bollingen Series, XXII (Princeton: Princeton University Press, 1969), p. 56.

5. Carl G. Jung, *Symbols of Transformation, Collected Works*, vol. 5, Bollingen Series, XX 2d ed. (Princeton: Princeton University Press, 1967), p. 183.

6. Jung, *Symbols of Transformation*, p. 368.

7. Ibid.

8. Sydney H. Mellone, "Gnosticism," *Encyclopaedia Britannica*, 16th ed. 10:453.

9. Jung, *Symbols of Transformation*, p. 376.

10. Kerényi, "The Primordial Child," p. 129.

11. Ibid., p. 123.

12. Neumann, *The Great Mother*, p. 176.

13. Mircea Eliade, "Mystery and Spiritual Regeneration in Extra-European Religions," in *Man and Transformation, Papers Selected from the Eranos Yearbooks* vol. 5, ed. Joseph Campbell, trans. Ralph Manheim, Bollingen Series, XXX (Princeton: Princeton University Press, 1964) p. 20.

14. Carl Kerényi, "Kore," in *Essays on a Science of Mythology* with Carl G. Jung, Bollingen Series, XXII (Princeton: Princeton University Press, 1969), p. 134.

15. Ibid., p. 138.

16. Ibid.

17. Ibid. pp. 143, 144.

18. Ibid., p. 142.

19. Jung, *Symbols of Transformation*, p. 277.

20. Ibid., 250.

21. George McMurray, "*Cumpleaños* y 'La Nueva Novela,'" in *Homenaje a Carlos Fuentes*, ed. Helmy F. Giacoman, (New York: Las Americas, 1971), p. 397.

Chapter VI

1. Roberto González Echevarría, "Carlos Fuentes. *Terra Nostra*; Cervantes o la crítica de la lectura," *World Literature Today* 52, no.1 (1978):84.

2. Fuentes's indebtedness to the movies, and particularly to radio, television and record players in the conception of *Change of Skin* (and in its execution) has been exhaustively documented by Fernando F. Salcedo in "Técnicas Derivadas del Cine en la Obra de

Carlos Fuentes" *Cuardernos Americanos*, 200 (1975):175–97. Similarly, Ronald Christ, in his article "Rhetorics of the Plot," *World Literature Today* 52, no. 1 (1978), characterizes Fuentes's technique in *Terra Nostra* as "cinematographic" understood as "manipulating the movement of movement." For Christ, too, Fuentes "replaces director, cameraman and editor in focusing our attention in an intermittent, flashing mode" (p. 39).

3. Carlos Fuentes, *Terra Nostra*, trans. Margaret S. Peden (New York: Farrar, Straus, Giroux, 1976), p. 533.

4. Carlos Fuentes, *Tiempo Mexicano* (Mexico D.F.: Joaquín Mortiz, 1972), p. 39. According to Fuentes, four distinct times or historic traditions coexist in Mexico: the indigenous mythic conception; the Roman tradition of legitimacy and continuity; Epicurean and Stoic individualism, which isolates one from the community; and rational positivism from England, France, and the United States, whose mask of morality hides its bourgeois class interests.

5. The attempted creation of a homunculus in the sixteenth century, impregnated with alchemical dreams of magic transformation which could "restore corrupted matter to purity" in the thought of Paracelsus, was not so bizarre an endeavor as would appear today. The recipe for homunculus making is given by André Malraux in *Les Voix du Silence* (Paris: Galerie de la Pléiade, 1951), p. 283. Like the fabrication of the "philosopher's stone," it was considered a secret process in which only the initiate could hope for success. Yet Isabel's royal corpses are not too different a matrix from the "magnetized" sperm from the bed of horse manure prescribed by Paracelcus.

6. Juan Goytisolo, "Our Old New World," *Review*, 19 (1976):10–13.

7. Michael Wood, "The New World and the Old Novel," *Inti* 5–6 (1977):112.

8. Carlos Fuentes, "La situación del escritor en América Latina," *Mundo Nuevo* I (1966):12.

9. Carlos Fuentes, "Noticia Necrológica" (unpublished manuscript, 1969) p. 27.

10. Pedro Gimferrer, "El Mapa y la Máscara," *Plural* 5 (1976):58.

11. Fuentes, *Tiempo Mexicano*, p. 24.

12. Mircea Eliade, "Mystery and Spiritual Regeneration in Extra-European Religions," in *Man and Transformation, Papers Selected from the Eranos Yearbooks*, vol. 5, ed. Joseph Campbell, trans. Ralph Manheim, Bollingen Series, XXX (Princeton: Princeton University Press, 1964), p. 21.

13. Juan-Eduardo Cirlot in *Diccionario de Símbolos* (Barcelona: Editorial Labor, S.A., 1959), p. 85, further suggests that the weaving and unravelling of the spider symbolizes continuous sacrifice through

which man is transformed throughout his existence. The idea of transfiguration in the map/mask symbol is also reinforced by Cirlot's explanation that the mask represents chrysalis, transfiguration from what one is to what one wishes to become; it is to facilitate the passing from one stage to another (p. 311). Thus, the map/mask symbol can be seen both to hide the past and to ease the passage into the future, that is to conceal one stage and reveal another.

14. Fuentes, to Duran, 8 December 1968 in the Appendix.

15. The prophetic faculties of the mirror as a symbol are also cited by Bettina Knapp in her study of Mallarmé, *Dream and Image* (New York: Whitston, 1977), p. 366. She says: "It was a hierophany, an aid to the discovery of the point of creation." In *The Prometheus Syndrome* (New York: Whitston, 1979), p. 229, the same author characterizes the mirror as a device used by Haller in Herman Hesse's *Steppenwolf* to reflect unconscious memories, to divest the hero of his ego and to fuse with a supraconsciousness, experiencing a vision of things beyond. (Is it literary influence or the collective unconscious that accounts for the fact that both Felipe and Hesse's Haller see a wolf in their future?)

16. Fuentes, *Tiempo Mexicano*, p. 15.

17. Ibid.

18. Ibid., p. 17.

19. Ibid., p. 21.

20. Ibid., p. 22.

21. Ibid., p. 12.

22. Ibid., pp. 39–40.

23. See especially Jung, Carl G., *The Integration of the Personality* (New York: Farrar and Reinhart, 1939).

Chapter VII

1. John Dwyer, "Una Conversación con Carlos Fuentes," in *Autorretratos y espejos,* ed. Gloria and Manuel Durán (Englewood Cliffs, New Jersey: Prentice-Hall, 1977), p. 63.

2. Carlos Fuentes, "Fortuna lo que ha querido," in *Cantar de ciegos,* (Mexico, D.F.: Joaquín Mortiz, 1970), p. 62.

3. See Plato, *The Symposium* (Hammondsworth, Middlesex: Penguin Books, 1951), p. 59. Aristophanes describes original man as follows: "each human being was a rounded whole, with double back and flanks forming a complete circle; it had four hands and an equal number of legs, and two identically similar faces upon a circular

neck, with one head common to both faces which turned in opposite directions. It had four ears and two organs of generation and everything else to correspond."

4. Carolyn Heilbrun, *Towards Androgyny*, (London: Victor Gollancz, 1973), p. xii.

5. Ibid., p. 58.

6. Juan-Eduardo Cirlot, *Diccionario de Símbolos*, (Barcelona: Editorial Labor, S.A., 1969), p. 75.

7. *Séraphita*, published by Honoré de Balzac in 1835, has as its central character Séraphita-Séraphitus, a perfect incarnation of all the spiritual virtues of both men and women, who is passionately loved by both a Norwegian shepherdess and a visiting intellectual male. But the love that Séraphita offers is not earthly love. He is all spirit and purifies those who come in contact with him.

8. Mircea Eliade, *Mephistopheles and the Androgyne* (New York: Sheed and Ward, 1965), p. 107.

9. The theme is discussed by Paz in *The Labyrinth of Solitude*, trans. Lysander Kemp (New York: Grove Press, 1961), especially in Chapter three. By Fuentes, it is discussed in *Casa con dos puertas* (Mexico: D.F.: Joaquín Mortiz, 1970), p. 173, where Fuentes in fact cites Mircea Eliade.

10. Eliade, *Mephistopheles*, p. 114.

11. Ibid., p. 117.

12. See the article by Severo Sarduy, "Un Fetiche de Cachemira," *Mundo Nuevo* 18 (1967):87–91.

13. Carlos Fuentes, *Holy Place*, trans. Suzanne Jill Levine in *Triple Cross* (New York: Dutton, 1972), p. 82.

14. Carlos Fuentes, *Change of Skin*, trans. Sam Hileman (New York: Farrar, Straus and Giroux, 1967), p. 138: "The dolls had a shocking peculiarity. All that were female had some male garment or characteristic; all that were male had something female . . . [on] the walls . . . paintings that were deformed and insane or obscene." In the description of Urs's painting, Fuentes speaks of "gaping mouths and terrified eyes," or "heaps of excrement, animals copulating, rotting snakes and elephants covered with swarms of flies."

15. Carl G. Jung, *Mandala Symbolism*, from *Collected Works*, vol. 9, part 1, Bollingen Series, XX (Princeton: Princeton University Press, 1972), p. 5. (paperback)

16. Carl G. Jung, *Psychology and Alchemy*, *Collected Works*, vol. 12, Bollingen Series, XX (Princeton: Princeton University Press, 1968), p. 41.

17. Edward Edinger, *Ego and Archetype* (New York: Putnam, for the C. G. Jung Foundation for Analytical Psychology, 1972), pp. 3–11, especially, p. 4.

18. Ibid., pp. 5, 9.

19. Ibid., p. 211; also see Jung, *Mandala Symbolism*, pp. 3–5.

20. Carl G. Jung, *Psychology and Religion, Collected Works*, vol. 11, Bollingen Series, XX (Princeton: Princeton University Press, 1969), pp. 59–63.

21. Edinger, *Ego and Archetype*, p. 182.

22. Jung, *Mandala Symbolism*, p. 3.

23. Ibid.

24. Befumo Boschi and Elisa Calabrese, *Nostalgia del futuro en la obra de Carlos Fuentes* (Buenos Aires: Fernando García Cambeiro, 1974), p. 82.

25. Adolphe Franck, *The Kabbalah*, (New York: Bell, 1940), p. 146.

26. Eliade, *Mephistopheles*, p. 118.

27. Edinger, *Ego and Archetype*, pp. 26–27.

28. Marcelo Coddou, "Terra Nostra o la Critica de los Cielos. Entrevista con Carlos Fuentes," *The American Hispanist* 3, no. 24, (1978):9. Fuentes says, "There is a confluence of oriental myths, Mediterranean myths and those of America which together depict a time which is no time, which is not purely original time, nor circular time, nor spiral time and has nothing to do with linear time, but one which portrays a kind of Mandala that contains all these possibilities and all the possible orientations in space."

29. Carl G. Jung, "Gnostic Symbols of the Self" in *Aion, Collected Works*, vol. 9, part 2, Bollingen Series, vol. 20 (Princeton: Princeton University Press, 1951), p. 207.

30. Carlos Fuentes, *Cervantes o la crítica de la lectura*, (Mexico, D.F.: Joaquín Mortiz, 1976), p. 43.

31. Note, for example, the fusion of religion and sex in the comparison of Aura to the crucified Christ: "You fall on Aura's nude body, on her open arms, stretched out from one end to the other of the bed, like the black Christ that hangs from the wall with his scarlet silk wrapped around his thighs, his knees open, his wounded side, his crown of thorns set on a tangled black wig with silver spangles. Aura opens up like an altar" (p. 56). Similarly in *Change of Skin*, the function of sexual love is psychic fusion: it is to "tie us to each other," to "destroy each other. To rob each of us of his solitary identity" (p. 329). Or again, "he transformed into your woman and you into his man in shared desire that was a fruit hanging to a single tree" (p. 323). For *Cumpleaños* see my article, "*Cumpleaños*, a Mythological

Interpretation of an Ambiguous Novel," *Latin American Literary Review* (1974):75–86. In this novel, the narrator says: "I stop being myself in order to be more myself; I stop being I in order to be they. I do not believe . . . that I possessed Nuncia; I was Nuncia" (p. 60).

32. My basic criteria for distinguishing these passages (which often share a certain sexual explicitness) from the final one in *Terra Nostra* as erotic rather than pornographic are that a love relationship precedes the sexual act, and that the emphasis in the descriptions is metaphysical rather than merely sexual. In *Terra Nostra*, however, the woman appears at the narrator's door as a stranger and he struggles against her: "you hold her away from you . . .you draw away from the kiss of the girl with tatooed lips . . .you draw away with repugnance. . . " (p. 774). But he finally allows himself to be seduced by her. This is as much a male fantasy as the appearance of the unknown Argentine woman in the bed of the painter in "Fortuna lo que ha querido" of *Cantar de ciegos*. In both the latter cases, the feeling of fusion has required no psychic or spiritual preparation on the part of the male partner. (Although the fashion of the times is to blend the erotic and pornographic, I believe that for literary criticism this distinction, although possibly subjective, must still be made.)

33. Franck, *The Kabbalah*, p. 106.

34. From an unpublished interview with Fuentes discussed by Emir Rodríguez-Monegal during a Yale University symposium on Mexico, 25 February 1978.

35. Fuentes, *Casa con dos puertas*, p. 254.

36. Fuentes, "Fortuna," p. 27.

37. This should not be confused with a sub-chapter "No hay tal lugar" in "Nowhere," *Cuerpos y ofrendas* (Madrid: Alianza Editorial, 1972), pp. 260–61. This chapter, with the change of the student's name, serves as verbatim model for the chapter, "Nowhere" in *Terra Nostra*.

38. Fuentes, *Cuerpos y ofrendas* (Madrid: Alianza Editorial, 1972), p. 11.

39. "El Dr. José Rodriguez Delgado, las ciencias biológicas, y el futuro de la humanidad," in *Autorretratos y espejos*, ed. Gloria and Manuel Durán (Englewood Cliffs, N.J.: Prentice-Hall, 1977), p. 166.

40. Heilbrun, *Towards Androgyny*, p. 342.

41. Eliade, *Mephistopheles . . .*, p. 100.

Chapter VIII

1. Anthony Burgess, "Mexican Thriller, *The Hydra Head*," *New York Times*, 7 January 1979, p. 11.

2. Carlos Fuentes, *The Hydra Head*, trans. Margaret Sayers Peden (New York: Farrar, Straus and Giroux, 1978).

3. Lanin Gyurko, "The Pseudo-liberated Woman in Fuentes's *Zona sagrada*," *Journal of Spanish Studies: Twentieth Century* 3 (1975): 40.

4. Richard Callan, "The Jungian Basis of Carlos Fuentes's *Aura*," *Kentucky Romance Quarterly*, 18 (1971):72.

5. Linda Hall, "The Ciplactli Monster: Woman as Destroyer in Carlos Fuentes," *Southwest Review*, 60 (1975): 246.

6. And they are all as faceless as Félix Maldonado, as the Mexican president he tries to face, or as Felipe Montero—all names without faces. They are all representatives of what Walter Sorell considers to be early man's desire for transformation, "for losing the identity of face and shape," and of a "contradictory need for self-repulsion as well as total possession of his self." The myriad of masks, doubles, and faceless characters with their De Chirico type of mask that populate Fuentes's works certainly testify to this ancient and ambivalent aspect of the human psyche. Facelessness and the mask betray an inner world that Fuentes is trying to conceal. Yet, as Walter Sorell concludes, "the mask is the beginning, trauma, and essence of all metamorphoses: it is the tragic bridge from life to death." "The Mystery of the Other Face," *M.D.*, September 1978, p. 11.

7. Quoted by Mulveen McKendrick in *Woman and Society in the Spanish Drama of the Golden Age*, (London: Cambridge University Press, 1974), p. 9.

8. Cited by Philip Rahv in *Literature and the Sixth Sense* (Boston: Houghton Mifflin, 1970), p. 213.

9. Ibid., p. 215.

10. Carlos Fuentes, "La situación del escritor en la América Latina," *Mundo Nuevo* 1 (1966):15.

11. Max Lüthi, *Once Upon a Time on the Nature of Fairy Tales*, trans. Lee Chadeayne and Paul Gottwald (Bloomington: Indiana University Press, 1976), P. 143.

12. Ibid. p. 115.

Bibliography

Major Works by Fuentes Cited in this Study

(in order of publication)

Los dias enmascarados. Mexico, D.F.: Los Presentes, 1954.

Where the Air Is Clear (La región más transparente). 1958. Translated by Sam Hileman. New York: Ivan Obelensky, 1960.

The Death of Artemio Cruz (La muerte de Artemio Cruz). 1962. Translated by Sam Hileman. New York: Farrar, Straus and Giroux, 1964.

Aura. 1964. Translated by Lysander Kemp. New York: Farrar, Straus and Giroux, 1965.

Cantar de ciegos. 1964. Mexico, D.F.: Joaquín Mortiz, 1967.

Holy Place (Zona sagrada). 3d ed. 1967. Translated by Suzanne Jill Levine. New York: Dutton, 1972.

Change of Skin (Cambio de piel). 1967. Translated by Sam Hileman. New York: Capricon Books, 1967.

Cumpleaños. Mexico, D.F.: Joaquín Mortiz, 1969.

Cuerpos y ofrendas. Madrid: Alianza Editorial, 1972.

Terra Nostra. 1975. Translated by Margaret Sayers Peden. New York: Farrar, Straus and Giroux, 1976.

The Hydra Head (La cabeza de la Hidra). 1978. Translated by Margaret S. Peden. New York: Farrar, Straus and Giroux, 1978.

Nonfiction, Letters, Essays by Fuentes

"La nueva novela Latinoamericana," *Siempre* 579 (1964):4.

"La situación del escritor en América Latina," *Mundo Nuevo* (1966):5–21 (dialogue with Emir Rodríguez-Monegal).

"*A Change of Skin,*" *New York Times,* 3 March 1968, section 7, p. 17.

Letters to Gloria Durán (included in the Apprendix), 8 December 1968 and 24 July 1969.

Casa con dos puertas. Mexico, D.F.: Joaquín Mortiz, 1970.

Tiempo mexicano. Mexico, D.F.: Joaquín Mortiz, 1972.

"Datos Biográficos," *Obras completas.* Mexico, D.F.: Aguilar, 1974.

Cervantes o la crítica de la lectura. Mexico, D.F.: Joaquín Mortiz, 1976.

Other Works Cited

Avellaneda, Andrés O. "Función de la complejidad en *Cambio de piel* de Carlos Fuentes." *Norte* 20, no. 2 (1969):21–27.

Baroja, Pio. *El árbol de la ciencia.* New York: Las Americas, 1957.

Bell, Gene. "*Terra Nostra* by Carlos Fuentes." *The New Republic,* 9 April 1977, pp. 30–32.

Boschi, Befumi, and Calabrese, Liliana and Elisa. *Nostalgia del futuro en la obra de Carlos Fuentes*. Buenos Aires: Fernando García Cambeiro, 1973.

Burgess, Anthony, "The Hydra Head," *New York Times Book Review*, January 1979, p. 11.

Bott, Francois. "Zone Sacrée." *Le Monde*, 10 August 1968.

Callan, Richard. "The Jungian Basis of Carlos Fuentes' *Aura*." *Kentucky Romance Quarterly* 18 (1971):65–75.

Carballo, Emanuel. *19 Protagonistas de la literatura mexicana del siglo XX*. Mexico: D.F.: Empresas Editoriales, S.A., 1965.

"Carlos Fuentes et les Sorcières," *Le Figaro Littéraire*, 30 January 1964, p. 2.

Caro-Baroja, Julio. *Vidas mágicas e Inquisición*. Vol. 2. Madrid: Taurus, 1967.

Caso, Alfonso. *La religión de los Aztecas*. México, D.F.: Secretaria de Educación Pública, 1945.

Castagnino, Raúl H. "Estado actual de la novela en Hispanoamérica." *Cuadernos del Sur*, 8–9 (1967–68): 129–36.

Christ, Ronald. "Rhetorics of the Plot." *World Literature Today* 52 (1978):38–44.

Cirlot, Eduardo. *Diccionario de Símbolos*. Barcelona: Editorial Labor, S.A., 1969.

Clive, Geoffrey, ed. *The Philosophy of Nietzsche*. New York: Mentor, 1966.

Coddou, Marcelo. "*Terra Nostra* o la Crítica de los Cielos." *The American Hispanist* 3, no. 24 (1978):9 (Interview with Carlos Fuentes).

De Guzman, Daniel. *Carlos Fuentes*. New York: Twayne Publishers, 1972.

Dubos, Rene. "Biological Individuality." *Columbia Forum* 20 (1969):5

Dwyer, John, "Una Conversación con Carlos Fuentes." *Autorretratos y espejos*. Edited by Gloria and Manuel

Durán. Englewood Cliffs, New Jersey: Prentice-Hall, p. 63.

Edinger, Edward. *Ego and Archetype.* New York: G.P. Putnam's Sons, for the C.G. Jung Foundation for Analytical Psychology, 1972.

Eliade, Mircea. *Mephistopheles and the Androgyne.* New York: Sheed and Ward, 1965.

———. "Mystery and Spiritual Regeneration in Extra-European Religions," in *Man and Transformation,* vol. 5, ed. Joseph Campbell, Bollingen Series, XXX (Princeton: Princeton University Press, 1964), pp. 3–36.

Franck, Adolphe. *The Kabbalah.* New York: Bell, 1940.

Frye, Northrop. *Anatomy of Criticism.* New York: Atheneum, 1969.

Gallagher, David. "*A Change of Skin.*" *New York Times,* 3 March 1968, section 7, p. 17.

———. "Stifled Tiger." *New York Times Book Review,* 4 February 1968, pp. 5, 40–41.

Gimferrer, Pere. "El Mapa y la Máscara." *Plural* 58 (1976):58–60.

Goytisolo, Juan. "Our Old New World." *Review* 19 (1976):5–24.

Gonzalez Echeverría, Roberto. "Carlos Fuentes' *Terra Nostra, Cervantes o la crítica de la lectura.*" *World Literature Today* 52 (1978):84.

Gyurko, Lanin. "The Pseudo-liberated Woman in Fuentes' *Zona sagrada.*" *Journal of Spanish Studies: Twentieth Century* 3 (1975):17–43.

———. "Freedom and Fate in Carlos Fuentes' *Cambio de piel.*" *Revista/Review Interamericana* 7, no. 4 (1977–78):703–39.

Graves, Robert. *The Greek Myths.* Vol. 2. Baltimore: Penguin Books, 1966.

———. "Ulysses." In *Homer, a Collection of Critical*

Essays, edited by George Steiner and Robert Fagles. Englewood Cliffs, N.J.: Prentice-Hall, 1962, p. 139.

Greeley, Andrew M. "There's a New-Time Religion on Campus." *New York Times Magazine*, 1 June 1969, pp. 14, 15, 17, 22, 26, 28.

Hall, Linda. "The Cipactli Monster: Woman as Destroyer in Carlos Fuentes." *South-West Review* 60 (1975):246–55.

Harris, Marvin. *Cows, Pigs, Wars and Witches*. New York: Random House, 1974.

Harss, Luis, and Dohmann, Barbara. *Into the Mainstream*. New York: Harper and Row, 1967.

Heilbrun, Carolyn. *Towards Androgyny*. London: Victor Gollancz, 1973.

Hill, Douglas, and Williams, Pat. *The Supernatural*. New York: Hawthorne Books, 1965.

Horowitz, Irving, ed. *The Anarchists*. New York: Dell, 1964.

Jung, Carl G. *Aion. Collected Works*, vol. 9, part 2. Bollingen Series, XX Princeton: Princeton University Press, 1959.

―――. *The Archetypes and the Collective Unconscious. Collected Works*, vol. 9, part 1. Bollingen Series, XX. Princeton: Princeton University Press, 1959.

―――. *The Integration of the Personality*. New York: Farrar and Rinehart, 1939.

―――. *Psychology and Religion*. New Haven: Yale University Press, 1938.

―――. *The Spirit in Man, Art and Literature. Collected Works*, vol. 15. Bollingen Series, XX. Princeton: Princeton University Press, 1966.

―――. *Symbols of Transformation. Collected Works*, vol. 5. Bollingen Series, XX. Princeton: Princeton University Press, 1956.

―――― and Kerényi, Carl. *Essays on a Science of*

Mythology. Bollingen Series, XXII. Princeton: Princeton University Press, 1969. paperback

Kafka, Franz. "The Silence of the Sirens." In *Homer, a collection of Critical Essays,* edited by George Steiner and Robert Faglos. Englewood Cliffs, N.J.: Prentice-Hall, 1962, pp. 98–99.

Kluger, Rivkah Schärf. *Satan in the Old Testament.* Evanston, Illinois: Northwestern University Press, 1967.

Knapp, Bettina. *Dream and Image.* New York: Whitston, 1977.

————. *The Prometheus Syndrome.* New York: Whitston, 1979.

Lévi-Strauss, Claude. *Anthropologie Structurale.* Paris, Plon, 1958.

Lüthi, Max. *One Upon a Time on the Nature of Fairy Tales.* trans. Lee Chadeayne and Paul Gottwald. Bloomington: Indiana University Press, 1976.

McCrary, William C. *The Goldfinch and the Hawk.* Chapel Hill, North Carolina: University of North Carolina Press, 1966.

McKendrick, Mulveen. *Woman and Society in the Spanish Drama of the Golden Age.* London: Cambridge University Press, 1974.

Mead, Robert. "Carlos Fuentes, Airado Novelista Mexicano." *Hispania* 1 (1967):229–35.

————. Carlos Fuentes, Mexico's Angry Novelist." *Books Abroad* 38 (1964):380–82.

Mellone, Sydney H. "Gnosticism." *Encyclopaedia Brittanica,* 16th ed, 10–455.

Murray, Gilbert. *Manual of Mythology.* New York: Tudor, 1935.

Paz, Octavio. *The Labyrinth of Solitude.* New York: Grove Press, 1961.

Peden, Margaret S. "*Terra Nostra,* Fact and Fiction." *American Hispanist* September, 1975, p. 4.

Plato. *The Symposium*. Baltimore: Penguin Books, 1951,
    pp. 32–114.

Rodríguez-Monegal, Emir. "El mundo mágico de Carlos
    Fuentes." *Número*, second series, 20 (1963):144–59.

Sarduy, Severo. "Un fetiche de cachemira." *Mundo
    Nuevo* 8 (1967):87–91.

Sommers, Joseph. *After the Storm*. Albuquerque, N.M.:
    University of New Mexico Press, 1968.

————. The Present Moment in the Mexican Novel."
    Books Abroad 40 (1966):261–66.

Sorrell, Walter. "The Mystery of the Other Face." *M.D.*,
    September 1978, p. 11.

Sykes, Gerald. *The Hidden Remnant*. New York: Harper,
    1962.

Toffler, Alvin. *Future Shock*. New York: Random House,
    1970.

Ullán, José Miguel. "Carlos Fuentes, Salto Mortal Hacia
    Mañana." *Insula* 22, no. 245 (1967):1, 12–13.

Wilson, S. R. *"La cabeza de la hidra," Journal of Spanish
    Studies, Twentieth Century* 7 (1979):107–10.

Wood, Michael. "The New World and the Old Novel."
    Inti 5–6 (1977):112.

Index

Adam, 214 n. 32
Alexander, Franz, 38
Andreev, Leonid, 127, 128
Androgyne, 112, 192; as seen
by Heilbrun, 170; in *Holy
Place*, 191; as seen by Jung,
172, 173, 177; in *Terra Nostra*, 163, 167, 169, 177. *See
also* Eliade, Mircea, on an-
atomical hermaphrodite
Anima, 31, 32; as agent of
transformation, 193; ambivalence of, 33, 63, 133, 155;
bipolarity of, 33; as Carlota
of Mexico, 48, 49, 209
n.8; in *Change of Skin*, 98,
100, 119; in "The Doll
Queen," 198, 199; as femme
fatale, 185; as femme in-
spiratrice, 33, 61; in *Holy
Place*, 80; in *Hydra Head*,
184, 185; immortality of, 34,
137, 155; relationship to
collective unconscious, 63;
relationship to reincarnation, 61, 62; relationship to
"shadow," 173; relation-
ship to time, 60, 100; relationship to wisdom, 64, 100,
133, 134, 156, 184; in *Terra
Nostra*, 161. *See also* Archetypal figures; Great
Mother; Terrible Mother
Animals in witchcraft: in *Aura*,
57; in *Holy Place*, 89. *See
also* Familiars; Sacrifice
Animus, 33
Apocalypse: as seen in *Change
of Skin*, 118, 126; in *Terra
Nostra*, 152, 166
Apollodorus, 75, 94
Archetypal figures, 31; danger of, 117; Fuentes's use
of, 36; relationship to religion, 126, 127, 136, 143,
173; in *Terra Nostra*, 150;
transmission of by heredity,
34
Archetypal Masque, 127, 128
Archetypal patterns: in Hag-
gard, 45 in James, 44; in
Pushkin, 44
Arrom, José, 217 n. 47
Avellaneda, Andrés, 214 n. 9